The
Garland Library
of
War and Peace

The
Garland Library
of
War and Peace

Under the General Editorship of

Blanche Wiesen Cook, *John Jay College, C.U.N.Y.*

Sandi E. Cooper, *Richmond College, C.U.N.Y.*

Charles Chatfield, *Wittenberg University*

On Two Fronts
Letters of a Conscientious Objector

by

Corder Catchpool

edited by his sister
with a foreword by
J. Rendel Harris,

and a preface by
George Lansbury

with a new introduction
for the Garland Edition by
John W. Chambers

Garland Publishing, Inc., New York & London
1972

Library of Congress Cataloging in Publication Data

Catchpool, Corder, 1883-1952.
    On two fronts; letters of a conscientious objector.

    (The Garland library of war and peace)
    Reprint of the 1940 ed.
    1. European War, 1914-1918--War work--Friends,
Society of. 2. Gt. Brit. Army. Friends' ambulance
unit. 3. Conscientious objectors--England--Personal
narratives. I. Title. II. Series.
D639.F9C38 1972   940.3'162   76-147635
ISBN 0-8240-0411-6

Introduction

Before he died atop a mountain in Switzerland, the gentle English Quaker Corder Catchpool spent a lifetime working for world peace. He did not achieve it, and he lived through two of the most devastating wars in history, but he fervently pursued the goal in a quest which led him to the battlefields of France, the prisons of Great Britain, the streets of Nazi Germany, and the bombshelters of London in the blitz. Catchpool refused to abandon his ideal, and he lived it as well as preached it. Not knowing how to quarrel, he tried always to understand the other side. He sought to convert men from evil through kindness rather than coercion. "Under his shyness and reserve," The [London] Times observed, "there lay exceptional friendliness and care for others, and the serenity that came from a simple and deeply held faith." His life and his writings demonstrated the vitality of the religious ideal of peace and brotherhood through love and understanding, even amidst the havoc of the twentieth century.

Born in 1883, the son of a Leicester solicitor, in a family which had been Quaker for generations, Catchpool attended Friends' schools in Leicester and then Sidcot when the family moved to the Isle of Guernsey. As a teenager attending meetings for worship, he became imbued with the Quaker dedication to peace and humanitarianism based upon the belief that something of God existed in every person. A spiritual revival swept through the Religious Society of Friends in the early twentieth century in England and young Catchpool became sincerely convinced of the meaning of religious experience and the teachings of Jesus Christ. The young man's faith helped sustain him after the drowning of two of his brothers in a squall off the English coast.

Catchpool first went to work as an apprentice engineer for the Great Eastern Railway, and by studying evenings he earned a degree in engineering from the University of London. Although he became Assistant District Locomotive Superintendent at Ipswich, he found no fulfillment in his work. Instead, he turned to social service.

During his apprenticeship in London, he had discovered the poverty of the industrial slums and had worked part-time at Toynbee Settlement House. His concern for life convinced him to become a vegetarian, which he remained until his death. Politically, after a brief affiliation with the Liberals, he joined the Independent Labour Party and as a Christian socialist voted its ticket at every election. At twenty-eight, he resigned from the railway company and went to work for the Quaker owner of a cotton mill in Darwen, near Manchester, as a resident engineer and supervisor of the welfare of the workers. There Catchpool played an important part in establishing and directing Greenfield Garden Village, a planned community for the millhands and their families.

When the war broke out in August 1914, Catchpool and his younger brother hurried back to England from a vacation in Switzerland, but the thirty-one-year-old Quaker could not concentrate on his tasks at the cotton mill. His conviction that war was contrary to the will of God and the teachings of Jesus ensured that he would not participate in the killing, but his belief in social service convinced him that he must help alleviate the suffering of his fellow man.

He decided "to go out there so that there may be one little milieu of love at any rate, amid the welter of hate," and after joining the Friends' Ambulance Unit he arrived in France in November 1914. For nineteen months, he worked at the battlefront, dressing the wounds of mangled soldiers and civilians, darting along the trenches with a stretcher, zig-zagging an ambulance down shell-pocked roads, and finally, in the work he most intensely disliked, issuing directives from behind a desk as the adjutant of the Quaker unit. He came under fire during the first German gas attack at the second battle of Ypres and at the battle of Mons. He received the Mons Star for his services to the wounded in that campaign, but, ironically, the medal arrived while he was incarcerated in an English prison as a conscientious objector.

When Parliament passed the Conscription Act in early 1916, the Society of Friends had declared against any service which would aid in the prosecution of the war. Increasingly convinced that his work helped men to return to combat and that he was contributing to the military machine, Catchpool resigned in May 1916 from the ambulance unit in order to return to what he called "the second front" and to campaign at home against the war. As he explained at his second court-martial, "at home men who stood for the same ideals as myself were being reviled as cowards and shirkers, and forced into the army against their principles. When some of them were sent to France and became liable to the death penalty, I hesitated no longer. It seemed to me more honest and more manly to take my stand with them, make public profession of my faith, and accept the consequences."

His faith was simple but intense; it had to be to carry him through the ordeal he faced. As he scribbled it down during this period, he concluded that "there seem two simple precepts which sum up the life of the Christian: his own life must be pure, strong, and courageous; and he must love all men. I often think that the whole may be summed up in one phrase − 'Be strong; be kind.' "

With his resignation, Catchpool forfeited his exemption from the draft, and he subsequently refused the decision of the Local Draft Tribunal directing him to noncombatant work. Considering this a compromise of principle, he took the absolutist position, refusing any work ordered by the military or conscription authorities. Ignoring his decision, the military bureaucracy drafted him into the Sixth Worcester Regiment, and arrested him as a deserter in January 1917 when he refused to report for duty and put on a soldier's uniform.

His first court-martial found him guilty and condemned him to three and one-half months at hard labor. When he finished his sentence and continued to refuse to obey military orders, he was tried and convicted again, and sentenced to two and one-half years in prison, a term which was reduced to six months because of his ambulance service at the front. Before the war ended, Catchpool was court-martialled four times and served a total of two years and three months in prisons at Wormwood Scrubs, Exeter, and Ipswich. He walked out of prison in April 1919 a free man. In its records, the army officially discharged him as a private.

The sensitivity of the young Quaker gave him perception, and a facile writing ability gave him the means, to describe his experiences during the war. His graphic accounts of his encounters on the battlefield and in the courts-martial were collected by his sister and first published in 1918 as On Two Fronts: Letters of a Conscientious Objector, Edited by his Sister. *As Rendel Harris, Catchpool's friend and former teacher, explained in his foreword to the*

INTRODUCTION

original edition, the letters were published to counter the public hostility toward the despised "conchies" and to show that such men were sincerely following their consciences and were not moral and physical cowards. The letters revealed a tender yet dedicated soul; and as Catchpool's friend and biographer, William Hughes, has asserted, they had a transforming and inspiring effect upon many of the people who read them.

But the two years in prison — most of it in solitary confinement, sitting alone on a stool twelve hours a day, denied books for the first year, and allowed only one letter a month — wore heavily upon the young Englishman. He was mentally and physically debilitated when he left his cell in 1919; he had lost several teeth, and developed both insomnia and a spasmodic need to change the position of his arms and legs which continued for the rest of his life. Yet his indomitable spirit prevailed; the authorities could not conquer it. It was revealed in the intimate letters he wrote to his mother each month from his cell and which were published in 1941 as Letters of a Prisoner for Conscience' Sake.

Corder Catchpool's conscientious objection against war did not end with the end of the war. He set out almost immediately for Germany, and from 1919 to 1921 he and his bride, Gwen Southhall, participated in the Quaker-directed project of feeding over one million German children each day in that war-ravaged country. During the 1920's, he returned to supervise

10

the community projects at the cotton mill village in Darwen, England, and until the program terminated with the depression of the nineteen-thirties, his home in the workers' village served as a hostel for German and French youths and as a haven during a brief visit by the Indian nonviolent revolutionary, Mohandas K. Gandhi.

In 1931, Catchpool moved to the Friends' International Center in Berlin. There he worked for reconciliation among Germany, England, and France; he sought to reduce the severity of the Versailles Treaty which he felt played into the hands of extreme nationalists like the Nazis, and he sponsored exchange groups among the three countries. Following Hitler's rise to power in January 1933, Catchpool aided a flood of Nazi victims — Social Democrats, Communists, and Jews — offering them asylum in the Quaker Center and helping them to flee across the borders. The Gestapo arrested him and questioned him for two days, but he refused to disclose the names of those whom he had assisted. Nevertheless, the experience convinced him of the need to understand what caused people to become Nazis, and as a result he studied their material and talked with them and sought to convince them of their error, from a position of human compassion. His willingness to talk to Hitler's followers led some to accuse him of being pro-Nazi, but he continued to aid the Nazis' victims and to plead, sometimes successfully, for the prisoners who had been sent to the forced labor camps.

He finally left Berlin in 1936 because of financial difficulties and the desire to remove his daughters from the increasingly Nazified German schools, but he returned many times during the late nineteen-thirties to work for reconciliation and to keep the lines of communication open among the nations of Europe. In the spring of 1937, he accompanied George Lansbury, the former leader of the British Labour Party, who as a pacifist resigned over the question of increasing armaments, on a personal goodwill mission to ease tensions between England and Germany. He was to have been Lansbury's interpreter in an interview with Hitler, but was replaced by a German at the last minute. Catchpool greatly sympathized with Lansbury's efforts to arrange a general peace conference among the nations and he also sought to bring Germany back into the League of Nations. Neither occurred, and instead both England and Germany rearmed, despite the pleas of pacifists like Catchpool and Lansbury. Increasingly in the late nineteen-thirties, Catchpool aided persecuted German Jews to emigrate and provided relief for them in England. Once again he found himself swept along in the drift to war.

Fifty-six years of age when World War II erupted in 1939, Catchpool spent the war years in England actively working to alleviate suffering. He became one of the leaders of the Bombing Restriction Committee which protested the saturation night bombing of *entire cities begun by the Royal Air Force in 1942, and he opposed the Allied food blockade of countries occupied by the Germans. At home, his World War I letters were republished in 1940 with a new preface by George Lansbury (the edition reprinted here), and his prison letters to his mother were published the following year. He personally counseled many conscientious objectors and visited absolutists in prison. During the bombing raids on London, he served as a stretcher-bearer and as a relief worker in the air-raid shelters of the East End. Although his own house was hit by a fire-bomb in 1944 and the top floor destroyed, none of the Catchpool family was injured.*

After the Second World War as after the First, he sought to aid the ravaged areas of Europe and helped organize relief for the millions of refugees torn from their homes. Once again he actively participated in the peace movement to prevent another war. A founding member of the British Peace Pledge Union in the nineteen-thirties, he was treasurer of the organization from 1944 through 1948. In the nineteen-fifties he devoted much of his time to his task as vice-chairman of the executive committee of the National Peace Council, the coordinating agency for the various peace societies in England.

In 1952, Catchpool was scheduled to return to Berlin to work against Cold War tensions when he and his wife decided to take a vacation and climb the 15,000-foot Monte Rosa, the highest mountain in

INTRODUCTION

Switzerland. The 69-year-old hiker soon became exhausted on the slopes, and on the second day of the ascent, his wife and his guide left him three thousand feet from the top and scrambled down to the village for help. When they returned, he was dead.

The memory of Corder Catchpool has remained alive, however, among those who knew him through his work or through his writings. From Germany, the chairman of the Association of Social Democrats praised his "deep ethical consciousness" and another friend, Julie Schlossen, wrote a commemorative work, Freundschaft mit einem englischen Quaker *(Hamburg, 1956). In England, his daughter, Jean Corder Greaves, wrote a biographical sketch which was published in 1953 as part of the* Quaker Biographies Series, *and his friend, William R. Hughes, produced a warm and thorough biography,* Indomitable Friend: The Life of Corder Catchpool, 1883-1952 *(London, 1956). The most fitting epitaph may have come from the British pacifist Vera Brittain who in a letter to* The Times *declared that "the memory of his integrity, courage, and sheer beauty of spirit will surely compel those who knew him to redouble their efforts to achieve the purposes for which he strove." Corder Catchpool would have asked no more; his ideal would be kept alive.*

November, 1971   John W. Chambers
                          Department of History
                  Mills College of Education, New York

14

ON TWO FRONTS

Letters of a Conscientious Objector

ON TWO FRONTS

Letters of a Conscientious Objector

By

CORDER CATCHPOOL

Edited by his sister
with a foreword by
J. RENDEL HARRIS, D.D.
and a new preface by
GEORGE LANSBURY

LONDON
GEORGE ALLEN & UNWIN LTD
MUSEUM STREET

First published by Headley Brothers Publishers, Ltd., 1918
Reprinted 1919
Third Edition 1940

PRINTED IN GREAT BRITAIN BY HEADLEY BROTHERS
109 KINGSWAY, LONDON, W.C.2 ; AND ASHFORD, KENT

CONTENTS

PREFACE TO THIRD EDITION

I HAVE been given the privilege of writing a short
foreword to this enthralling book—enthralling because
it is a clear record of the working of a man's mind, a mind
dominated by the one overriding thought that the " Way
of Life " as taught by Jesus, is the only way of life that
can bring peace to individuals and nations. You must
read this record for yourselves, if you would understand
the vital difference between voluntary service on behalf
of God and the people and compulsory service attempted
to be forced upon men whose whole conception of life is
based on the eternal truth, that our minds and conscience
belong to ourselves and God and not to the State, however
the State is constructed or governed.

Corder Catchpool served in the Friends' Ambulance
Unit from November 1914 until May 1916, when he
became convinced the coming of Conscription would
mean for him and his friends compulsory service in a
military machine. So he came home leaving the fighting
front where his colleagues and himself had faced death
and all the horror of war striving to alleviate suffering,
and giving as far as this is possible, comfort and consolation
to the dying.

Coming home brought him into the company of those
who were facing moral, mental and material problems on
another kind of front. We can all understand and appreciate the selfless heroism and consequent suffering and loss
sustained by men and boys who serve in the Forces on
land, sea and air. It is in our blood to sympathize with
their loved ones who bear a heavy load of hourly anxiety,
lest those they love the best on earth may never return.

This struggle of conscientious objectors on the " Home Front " cannot, because of its very nature, carry the same kind of almost universal grief and loss. I venture to believe that Corder Catchpool and his friends, although not enduring the same kind of loss and suffering, did suffer intense mental and spiritual worry when finding themselves compelled to give up an active voluntary service on behalf of the sick, wounded and dying in Belgium and France, and become " Passive Resisters " against laws which, if obeyed by them, would violate all their most cherished beliefs and faith.

To-day, 25 years after the first of the events recorded in this book took place and 20 years after the war officially ended, the same struggle which Corder Catchpool and his friends engaged in is taking place throughout the length and breadth of our country. This would seem to prove how futile are the sacrifices made by C.O.s in the last war and this.

I cannot believe this will be the case. I write as one who dares not say what he would, or would not do if he were young, except, I might die or suffer, but would never kill for my faith. My conviction is that although there is a mass of untold suffering, misery and loss now being endured and still to come, there is growing up an intense longing for a better way of life. It is a terrible disaster that for the months past leaders of Christian Churches accept and support this horrible tragedy of war. It is also something to be thankful for that all Christians as well as non-Christians, unite in declaring war cannot settle anything, and the vast majority who think do recognize the right of C.O.s to be heard and also to be exempted from taking part in killing. So I hope this record of four years' service will help all who tend to understand what the words " Conscientious Objector " really mean and also teach us all, more and more, to turn to Him of whom it was said " Thou hast the words of eternal Life," and learn from Him how to obtain courage and strength to follow Truth wherever it may lead us. One personal word in conclusion. I knew of Corder Catchpool and his friends during the Great War. I met him intimately when preparing for my visit to Herr Hitler in April 1937. His advice and encouragement were invaluable to me in drafting the memorandum I sent to the Führer a couple of weeks before leaving England. Corder came with me to Berlin. His knowledge of the officials and people generally and his readiness to overcome difficulties and to understand my troubles and anxieties made him not only a valuable adviser, but a friend in the best sense of the word. In company with Percy Bartlett it is possible to say although we were not " Three Musketeers " we were three friends striving to discover how to reach the inner recesses of Herr Hitler's mind. I am sure there is much more work of a similar character for him to do. I hope this book will be widely read so that people may better understand why men refuse to kill.

GEORGE LANSBURY

FOREWORD

THE little volume before us contains the letters and discloses the experiences of a young friend of mine, and one of my own students, during the momentous days of this Great War.* To me, at least, they have a charm of their own and a message of their own : the charm which comes from simplicity of speech wedded to elevated thought and sincere devotion ; and the message which they bring to us not to despair of the highest Republic of all, the Kingdom of God, even when it appears to be deserted by all except a handful of enthusiasts.

These letters are " good copy " in more senses than one ; no one will read Corder Catchpool's experiences with the ambulance at the front, and desire for himself or for others any other brand of courage or of calmness than is there disclosed. We may all wish to be as steady and as brave, as tenacious of our ideals, and as brimful of compassions. But most people will cease to admire or to wish to imitate, when they find that in the middle of the tale that is told, the scene changes abruptly from a French battlefield to an English detention cell. Inexplicable conduct on the part of a man who has evidently been " saved from all his fears " ! Corder Catchpool must tell us himself why and how he came to see that he must return to England, and take his stand with those who were fighting for the " right of self-determination " of small groups in great communities, the " contemptible little army " of those who thought freedom was the first and greatest thing for which they had to stand, and who were determined to save from

* i.e. 1914-1918 (Note to new edition).

Prussianism both the country of their birth and the Churches of their adhesion. Perhaps as we read these pages we shall get a glimpse of the Light that such men are following, and be able by analysis to determine whether it is the last and worst of Humanity's Will-o'-the-Wisps, or the Light that comes from the very Sun of Righteousness Himself, from whose wings the healings are to drop upon the discords of the Nations.

RENDEL HARRIS

THE OUTBREAK OF WAR

WE had tramped from Chamounix, hovering for a fortnight about the snow-line, when one evening we dropped down into Zermatt over the Theoduljoch. We had almost lost count of days, for time flows gently in the Valais, and we had learned to appreciate the one-handed clocks in the quaint church steeples of those picturesque Rhone-side hamlets.

"Diplomatic relations between Austria and Servia strained!" We rebelled a little at this sudden intrusion of the world of politics, and speedily as might be shook from us the dust of civilization and climbed up to the snow again. We had nearly finished our "work" and were to jog back quietly over the Furka and the Klausen to Schaffhausen, and so by the Rhine to Rotterdam and home.

At Hospenthal we were shaken rudely out of our dream. In the gloaming, when the gossips gathered, and the beer began to circulate, mine host of the "Goldener Stern" took down his fiddle and essayed a tune for the usual country dance. But his heart seemed too sad to make music, and his children clung about him, and he hung his fiddle up again. Next morning he was off to the mobilization with his rucksack on his back—"*à la guerre*" he said as he waved us good-bye, but knew not why he went.

All down the lovely Reussthal we tramped, and the pines, and the white winding ribbon of road and the green foaming torrent, and the eternal hills tossing up and up to the snow, were bathed in the gentle sunlight of a Sunday afternoon. The anxiety of some unknown trouble stabbed into the peace of the valley and into the peace in our hearts ; troop trains thundered down, and bayonets flashed at the loop tunnels, viaducts and stations of the wonderful railway. At Altdorf the little French *femme-de-chambre* was in tears. Her father and brothers will have to fight—"*je rêve, je rêve,—mais ce n'est pas une rêve !* . . .

13

ils sont forts, ils sont forts, les Allemands ! " " I want to go
to sleep and wake again when the war is over " ; and then
" *der Kreig, der Krieg !* " she cried, mixing languages in
her grief. We diverted our course to Lucerne—no longer masters
of the situation. A wild storm broke over the usually
placid lake, with fierce lightning and thunder and sheets
of rain, and from the Seelisberg they were sending up
rockets to guide the " *Schiller* " out of the dangerous
Urnersee. Gloom, too, reigned in our minds, and over
Europe we feared loomed a storm infinitely more dreadful
than that lashing the green waters of the Vierwaldstättersee.
The lake boats were already running to a reduced " *Kriegs-
fahrplan*", and on board the Swiss refused their own five
franc notes in payment of fare.

At Lucerne we found an anxious crowd staring at a
notice on the door of the British Consulate—" The British
Consul and Vice-Consul being away on military service,
British visitors must apply to the Consul at Zurich, or the
Ambassador at Berne." Every bank, open for reduced
hours only, was besieged by a large disorganized queue in
which we waited with the hope of being able to change the
five pound note refused at our last hotel. It had all come
upon us so suddenly—as yet we had seen no newspapers,
and already for days neither letters nor any foreign communication had come through. In the meantime, as we
waited in the crowd, scraps of news illuminated vaguely
the general obscurity, yet assuring us only too plainly
that our worst fears were in the way of being realized.
In the prevailing ignorance conversation became some-
what wild. People were talking of the end of the world
(in which case, said someone drily, it was not much use
waiting in a crowd for money), the degree of painfulness
in death from a bayonet thrust, or the relative disadvantage
of being killed by a German in Britain, or by a Jap in the
States.

We heard many a tale of hardship from those who had
come through from England a day or two before, left

stranded at the frontier, without food, shelter or any immediate means of further transport, amid the crowds clearing the frontiers in all directions, to regain their own countries.

At last I was one of the fortunate three to gain admission in one of the momentary openings of the door, and more to the point than much vague talk, was the cashier's curt reply :—" Yes, 120 francs Swiss paper." Nothing to do but close with the bargain, poor as it was, at once ; and right glad were we too, for after that day no five pound Bank of England note was changed by the Lucerne banks for over a week. As the day wore on our situation became clearer. There was only one possible means of leaving the country—by way of Italy. With the wild impulse to be moving we hurriedly considered the prospect of working our passage home by ship from Genoa ; but further advice from the most authoritative quarters counselling delay, reluctantly we renounced the thought of a night dash through the St. Gothard, and all the afternoon, in the rain, our dismal duty was to hunt round the town for the cheapest lodgings. At length we found a little Weinstube, where the modest *pension* we were almost ashamed to offer was not disdained ; and thereupon we settled ourselves down as patiently as might be to wait.

The tale of many days is now quickly told. Some of them were fine, some were wet ; violent thunder-storms were frequent, but we no longer cared about the weather, nor looked anxiously for tints of red in the sky at sunset. A meeting of British subjects in the Kursaal raised our spirits a little, but for days nothing more was heard. We had to husband to the utmost our slender resources, and counted the days that remained before they should be exhausted. Hundreds were in the same plight, and some in worse. We heard of an English clergyman and his wife who had not a franc between them. And everywhere there were soldiers. Soldiers with fixed bayonets guarding the railway station and refusing all admission ; guarding the post office, and allowing entry one at a time to the long queue waiting to send telegrams, at treble the usual rates, in French, German or Italian only, and doubtful of delivery. Drilling proceeded under the falling rain on all open spaces, and, sodden, the patient men marched off to entrain for the concentration in the North. Then came the awful news that our own country was mobilizing—then that she was at war, and the whole ghastly picture seemed complete. And all we could do was just to wait. The *ennui* of it—the sickening horror of the thought of the great tragedy, and here the mocking, sunlit waters of the lake, the pure snow on the Titlis and the Todi yonder, beyond the pine-fledged cliffs that drop sheer into the green depths of Lucerne.

One stirs a moment to the strains of martial music, and sees but the same bronzed men marching—no enthusiasm there or amongst the populace—two hundred thousand conscripts away North to the lowlands, where the great mountain barriers soften into hills, and powerful neighbours drunk with blood may violate the neutrality of this kindly, peaceful, welcoming little country. So her manhood has to go—" *Mon mari est parti ce matin*," says our hostess with a sob, and her little girl plays disconsolately with baby, well knowing that something is amiss. Away in Hospenthal we have seen another afflicted home ; and how many, like the little *femme-de-chambre* at Altdorf, would fain sleep till the war be over, that this horror may not pass before their waking eyes. And so away they go marching in the rain or the sun—it is all the same—officers with bare sword blades touching here or there a man upon the shoulder, who does not carry well the great load upon his back.

A number went off this afternoon. Dusty and hot with a long tramp from some country camp ground, they marched with flying colours and bands playing through the town, an occasional dog-like yelp—the Swiss makeshift for a cheer—emphasizing the passiveness rather than the enthusiasm of the people. For some time they stood easy on the great Bahnhofplatz, rifles stacked and the heavy kit slung down from their shoulders. Perspiration streamed from their faces, and at the opened shirt-collar one could see the little plaque bearing the soldier's name and home suspended on the hairy chest. Wives and sweethearts and children pressed eagerly around, and one hoped they did not catch the significance of those little plaques. The ambulance divisions, with boxes and stretchers were there, and the news ran that hostilities had broken out on the Swiss frontier, and that reserve divisions were being hurried North. The rifles rattled again, the tambours took up the time, away marched the troops to the trains waiting close by, and, the little incident over, we went back to our efforts at killing time.

One tried to shake off the *ennui*—the brooding over gloomy thoughts. We walk into the fields, where women and aged men are getting in the hay, and beg to help them at their work. Many cannot understand our German, and some say that the work is done, distrustful perhaps of subjects of one of the great nations whose jealousies and ambitions have brought all this trouble upon an innocent people. Once the opportunity did come—a quaint old figure, bent almost double under a large straw hat, spoke to us as we sat by the roadside. All her men folk were away—the haycrop yonder had to be stored in the loft. And so through the hottest hours of the day we worked for her and rejoiced, and at the end she combed the hay out of her " children's " hair, and wiped the perspiration from their faces, and poured out her good red home-made wine. But the privilege of helping was not again to be ours.

We climb the Sonneberg and look away to the great rampart of the Juras—behind which more soldiers are marching up from the East, and from the West, through the vineyards of the Saone and the Rhine—men from the German homesteads, from the villages of France, marching up to die. The mountains cannot hide from our thoughts the tragedy that is upon the world. There is the sting of exile—nothing to do—no certainty—and the horror beating round one's brain moment by moment.

Even at lovely Lucerne to be patient is hard. We dare spend literally nothing. For just one week now we have bought one newspaper at ten centimes per day, and once, with glorious extravagance, sixty centimes went upon a cake of soap. More we dare not do. And yet there is no sign of relief. With monotonous iteration the official report still states, " There is at present *no* chance of returning home." The same veil still hangs close drawn upon the future. We have nothing to read. At Chamounix there were two wet days, and we bought a novel. We are reading it through to each other for the third time. It is fearfully hot and enervating, and walking in the daytime has become almost impossible. For some time we slept abundantly, but now that chiefest mercy is being denied us, and restless nights follow restless days.

There has been another meeting of English exiles in the Kursaal. A strong committee has been formed, with offices, and a fund opened for the relief of severe distress, so the worst anxiety is over. Some fifteen hundred were present, and the meeting brought great relief. I think the English service, too, was a great help to many. It was deeply impressive, and the church was full to overflowing. There was a sudden pregnant hush before we prayed " Give peace in our time, O Lord," and one of the Psalms for the day must have struck all present as peculiarly appropriate :—

" God is our refuge and strength, a very present help in trouble. Therefore will we not fear though the earth be moved. . . . He maketh wars to cease in all the world. Be still and know that I am God."

The New Testament lesson was the eighth chapter of Romans, and Canon Allison took for his text the " Quis separabit ". Then we sang " O God our help in ages past ", and trooped out into the sunshine.

*   *   *   *

We have been waiting for eleven days. This morning comes news from the Ambassador at Berne that it will be

at least a week before the first official train can get through
—a month before all the English waiting to return home
can be conveyed thither. There is another news item :
Two young men who were prepared to take some risks
have got through to London. Why should not we be the
second two ? Besides, to-day the first newspapers have
come through from the outside, betokening, like Noah's
dove, that the waters of isolation are abating. We have
had a busy day making arrangements, going through all
sorts of passports and other formalities, and buying in
provisions for three days. The relief to be *doing* something
at last ! To-morrow morning we are off àt 6.30 to Berne,
to see the French Ambassador ; on to Lausanne, and next
day, for better for worse—away.

* * * *

I write this last word from a Lancashire cotton town.
Old England ! the comfort of your calm after the indescrib-
able turmoil of half a continent ! There was not danger as
we had been told there would be ; only pain of mind,
waking the weary body, and refusing rest to eyes a-smart
for want of sleep. That never-to-be-forgotten journey—
lovely France dreaming under summer sun and starry sky,
infinitely pathetic—is a story in itself, and I may not tell
it now, for must we not try to be cheerful ?

THE CALL TO THE FRONT

EDITOR'S NOTE.—The " pain of mind " which Corder
Catchpool experienced during the early days of mobilization in Switzerland, was felt still more poignantly, when,
coming home through North-Western France, he met the
first drafts of the British Army passing through Amiens on
their way to meet the enemy at Mons. Of this sorrow and
anguish of mind there had already been born a desire and
determination to go, if possible, into the firing zone, to
relieve the physical suffering and to maintain a spirit of
Love in the midst of the rising tide of hatred. Nearly
two years later he wrote to a friend, " When the present
war broke out, the horror of it seemed at times more than
I could bear. Believing that war is contrary to the will of
God, as revealed in the life and teaching of Jesus Christ,
and that it is possible to live in a spirit of love that takes
away the occasion of all war, I was unable to enlist or bear
arms, either for offence or defence. Within a few days,
however, I had experienced a call to take up ambulance
work, should the way open. There was a cry for voluntary
helpers ; I believed there might be great opportunities for
service, rendered in the spirit of the Prince of Peace, in
tending the wounded and dying, amongst whom I saw
moving the figure of Him I strive to follow."

The opportunity to equip himself for this service came
with the formation of a group of young men of the Society
of Friends, who banded themselves together to undergo a
course of training for Red Cross and Ambulance work.
To this end a camp was established at the Quaker Hostel
called Jordans in Buckinghamshire, and there a thorough
course of training was carried through. The camp
terminated with a route march to Cambridge, after which
C.C. wrote to a friend :—

*   *   *   *

18th October, 1914.

Camp was disbanded yesterday evening on our return from Cambridge, and, as promised, we now have in our hands papers giving particulars of three fields of service where help is urgently needed—help which we are now qualified to give. . . . I think probably I shall go to France, with the transport party, but in that case I shall have to wait a week or two. Meanwhile there is any amount of work to be done. On Tuesday I am going up to the London hospital for a week's dressing practice, and shall be living at Toynbee Hall. I have got through two inoculations for typhoid without much trouble, which is a relief—the population of my body being increased by 1,500,000,000 ! I have to undergo vaccination this week for the third time in my life.

THE FIRST WINTER

1st Anglo-Belgian Field Ambulance,*
Malo-les-Bains,
Nord,
9th November, 1914.

I SHALL never forget that day we left for France. Right up to late the evening before I had lingered over operations at the hospital. I couldn't bear to leave the dear old " London "—I shouldn't be surprised if I came to number that fortnight in " Out-patients " amongst the septic dregs of East End humanity with the happiest of my life : for beyond the joy and interest of the immediate work, there was that sense of preparation—of moving on a swift current to something sublime, if only one might prove big enough and faithful enough. So *the* day was such a rush as even beat all *my* previous records. For five solid hours of it, I was dashing about London in a taxi, buying and collecting kit, beginning with the sleeping bag, into which everything else tumbled, from morphia tablets to campaign boots— a soldier's packing. Finally to the outfitter's in Regent Street, to pack my *person* into khaki ! Then paraded and marched thirty strong, to Charing Cross, chanting the inevitable " Tipperary ".

In the train identity discs were distributed, little things to sling round your neck, to know you when you're dead. Evening brought " Specials ", palpitating with Battle of the Dunes ; and our luggage booked through to Dixmude, so to speak ! Then night—a bit in the middle of it—at the old Naval canteen in Dover—pickled onions, polony and black coffee at midnight—first experience of sleep in our patent bags on the dirty floor boards—bleak dawn, the Quay with the *Invicta* alongside and the little " Mors "

* Afterwards known as " The Friends' Ambulance Unit ", and generally referred to as the " F.A.U."

'buses slinging aboard. Then came heavy swell, fading cliffs, reverie. What a farewell to old England ! (Sentiment rather jealous these twenty-four hours past getting its own back !)

Our destroyer escort port and starboard suddenly shot ahead, burying themselves in smoke and drenching us with soot. Soon they were on the horizon east'ard leaving us *un*escorted, and crammed with cordite and 12-in. shells for the monitors. The *Invicta* was quivering forward under " every ounce " too, and eyes straining ahead detected meteoric strokes with black nucleus radiating *inwards* from all the compass-points. There in mid-channel was an assembly of torpedo flotilla—aye, and a cruiser down by the stern in the middle of 'em. The sea was strewn with bobbing *débris*—mostly petrol cans and human heads, from the old *Hermes*, torpedoed aft, and with poop awash already. The sudden sighting of a periscope shook us into pattern like the bits in a kaleidoscope, *Hermes* and *Invicta* in the middle, and the destroyers racing round in a ring, stem to stern—sort of nursery romp on the high seas, and I leaning over the rail with mind running on cordite and periscopes and the pity of losing eight brand new Mors ambulances ! The unit paraded on deck—we were out to a man, though the line was wobbly with sea-sickness. We were allotted a boat— a big honour and first job for the unit. Such of us as have the *pied marin* were selected to man her with Hector, an old sea dog who's doubled the Horn on a "wind jammer", captaining. We fished up a score or so of bobbing heads and got them aboard the *Invicta* on stretchers lowered from the deck by ropes. The ship was rolling so that there was danger of crushing the boats under the bilge-keel. I got my hand crushed rather badly, didn't notice the pain until I was endeavouring to grip a drowned seaman's slimy tongue. For an hour or more we were busy " *schafering* ". Saved all but three of the twenty we picked up. Meantime ——— dived overboard after someone and got his man. At last, nearly exhausted, we were free to go on deck again, and found the *Invicta* just under weigh, heading for Dover. The *Hermes'* great ram was sticking up vertical close alongside, and the destroyers were making out along their radii again. Then as the sun came out and the sea grew quieter we sat down and watched the old cruiser sink slowly to its long rest.

After carrying our patients quietly ashore at Dover and placing them in the summoned ambulances, we turned about again, made an uneventful voyage, and lay-to off Dunkerque about 7 p.m., waiting the tide. There was a glorious sunset, but we could hear the boom of the monitors up coast and the air was sown with homing biplanes. As soon as we got alongside they asked for immediate volunteer dressers ; hundreds of wounded at the station, and no one to attend to them. I am not rated as a dresser, but was mad to go—and *went*—got round a Doctor somehow—I believe I was almost irresistible just then. I shall never in my life forget the sight and sounds that met us. Figure two huge goods sheds, semi-dark, every inch of floor space—quais, rails, everywhere covered with the flimsy French stretchers, so that in places you had to step on them to get about—and on each stretcher a wounded man—desperately wounded, nearly every one. The air heavy with the stench of putrid flesh, and thick with groans and cries. 400 of these wounded, and one French medical student to attend to them—an English staff officer and an English naval officer helping voluntarily. Half dead as we were with fatigue, we flung ourselves into this work throughout the night, the need was so great. Consider this man, both thighs broken, and he has travelled twenty kilometres, *sitting on the seat* of a crowded railway carriage. Or this one, with his arm hanging by a shred of biceps—or this, with bits of bone floating in a pool of pus that fills up a great hole in his flesh, laughing bitterly when I turn away to vomit, overcome by the stench of sepsis—he may well laugh bitterly—he has lain eight days on the filthy floor in an outhouse of some farm near the front. Of all these, case after case

with bullet wound through the abdomen, septic, fatal—
so we work on through the night, hurrying from one to the
next, *et toi, où as tu été blessé? Balle? Eclat d'obus?* Ah, and
only able to touch a fringe. The priests touch more than
we, hurrying through the solemn rite—they need, men are
dying on all sides. At dawn we began loading the hospital
ships—carrying the wounded out to our ambulances,
running them down to the Quay, and carrying them aboard.
We worked most of the day loading, for when the sheds
had emptied, trains began to run through to the Quay—
cattle waggons and box goods vans, filthy dirty, twelve
stretchers apiece, packed like tinned fish. Frightfully
awkward to unload, especially the upper tiers, you can't
help knocking against these poor broken limbs often, and
the shriek pierces your heart—*you*'ve done it. Sometimes
you get a van *not* stretcher cases—crammed all the same,
men squatting on the floor, leaning against the sides. I
shall never forget the sight of a blinded German, last man
to leave the truck. The French N.C.O. shouted to him
to get out, and he sprang up staggering towards the open
door and that drop of several feet on to the stones, arms
sweeping the air in front, and I just saved him from falling.
The St. Martin's Summer midday heat was pitiless, and
my eyes smarted with fatigue. At length came a lull
and we got a delicious tea on the boat, and then lay down
on the cushions, but were soon dragged up out of heavy
sleep—another train in—Belgians this time. A friendly
brancardier gave me a French, German and Belgian bullet
for a "souvenir". I accepted them eagerly, but have
already passed them on—wrenched out the rootlet of this
poisonous souvenir habit—I have not come out to collect
the nucleus of a museum—*nor* to drive bargains out of this
devil's work of war. My *brancardier* couldn't tell me the
meaning or origin of "Boche". He said the Belgian
version was "Allboche", but that put me no forrarder.
At 7 p.m. we paraded on the Quay, and marched three
kilometres, to Malo, where quarters had been got for us at
the Hotel du Kursaal. All dog tired, you may guess, but

after a meal I implored the O.C. to let some of us go down to the sheds again for the night. The thought of that groaning sea of tortured men was almost more than I could stand. The O.C. was adamant—we must take rest, perhaps he was right ; he had responsibility. I thought him heartless. . . . We've been here over a week now, and things are straightening out a bit after that blind rush at the beginning. Besides the orderly work at H.Q., regular eight-hour shifts of dressers have been organized at the " Shambles ", as the goods sheds here have been christened. Drivers and cars are kept busy changing over the *équipes*, provisioning, etc. These huge sheds are filling and emptying every twenty-four hours. The town is a distributing centre—some trains run right through, without unloading—but most empty into the sheds (*triage*), and the wounded are sorted and shipped from the port to Cherbourg, Brest, Nantes, Bordeaux. It's pitiable to see them crowding the decks—no accommodation below, these bitter nights—dreading the sea, too. We never get more than a few hours' sleep at a time, our work is to re-dress the wounds ; most have been several days with only the first field dressing—filthy at that—and are frightfully septic. The priests glide about in the semi-darkness ; they always " administer " in cases of doubt, to be on the safe side—so that the man shall be, I mean—after which the chances are he turns over and dies—bad psychology !

Half these cases will lose a limb ; perhaps the blinded men are the saddest, if one excepts those who have gone mad. If one could grasp it, or stopped to think, one would be in danger one's self—the work is one's safeguard, and the need of help so urgent that I have never tasted purer happiness than during the past week. That English staff officer said on our first night at the Shambles, " You'll never go up to the front when the need here is so great?" —so we stay ; our ideal as a voluntary unit is just to fit in where the pressure comes on overworked or inadequate staffs. The poor men are so grateful for the little service one can render—sometimes it is merely to make them more comfortable to die, or the even humbler service of making them a little cleaner; you can imagine the joy of seeing clean white bandages replace filthy rags, and knowing that underneath wound or flesh has been bathed clean with antiseptic lotion. Besides various scissors, forceps, lint, bandages, surgeon's gloves, *eau-oxygenée*, *teinture d'iode*, and other medical necessaries, my little haversack goes down crammed with chocolate and cigarettes—especially the latter. See the *piou-piou's* face light up at sight of a " *cigarette Anglaise* ". The joy of striking a match, holding it to the cigarette (which you've probably had to place between the lips) and hearing those contented puffs ! There are all sorts, mostly French, Turcos, Zouaves, Arabs, coal-black Senegalese and an occasional stray Belgian, English, Indian, who has drifted out of his proper stream, which flows through Calais for the Belgians, Boulogne for the British Army. There is a good sprinkling of Germans too, one has to help the latter mostly by stealth, but it is lovely to be able to do so now and then. They are, of course, prisoners of war, and we are not free to do as we like. The French are apt to be very jealous. Their wounds are the most frightful of all—sometimes they have lain a week without any attention at all. They are very brave and do not seem to expect any kindness or attention. They suspect the drink one offers them, and often need a lot of persuading before one can touch their wounds.

* * * *

The only excitement is an occasional Taube raid, with the firing at it—machine guns and rifles mostly. I don't think they do a bit of " good ", but they are introducing anti-aircraft field pieces. The air is often thick with French 'planes at the time of such visits, but I have never seen them give chase to a German. Heavy firing (Dixmude-Ypres) is to be heard in the distance. I cannot often write. Typhoid is getting rife, and the danger of poison from septic wounds is always present (you know I have special reason to fear it),* so what with heavy work and little sleep it is vitally important to take all the rest possible. I am tired out now with a long day of twelve-and-a-half hours' work and may be called out again at midnight !

We have established a base hospital here at Dunkerque, and a dressing station at Ypres, at present under heavy shell fire. We are starting other dressing stations along the front, and the staffs will change periodically with those at the Base, so as to diminish the strain. I have not been out to the firing line yet, but shall be glad and happy to take my turn there when the time comes. I often watch the streams of cars that pass the Kursaal, thick with dust (in November !). The other day I asked a French soldier if they were going to the " Champ-de-bataille " ? " 'Y en a ", he replied, and somehow that laconic answer sticks in my mind, and makes me long to be away there too !

On Sunday evening I went with two of the doctors to the English Church service. There is an English chaplain (Irish, strictly speaking !) and a normal English congregation of some forty—but all have fled. The chaplain is " carrying on", however, with a mere two or three. Still, we know that is adequate ! On reaching the Church, we found the minister and congregation just leaving it. The gas wasn't functioning, and they proposed to abandon the service. We spoke our disappointment, quickly borrowed candles from kindly neighbours, and worshipped each with his candle lighted and *not* under a bushel—stuck with wax, in fact, upon the pew back just in front of him ! whilst up in the pulpit the chaplain had a " lampe-à-petrole ". We sung,

> " And then for those our dearest and our best,
> By that prevailing Presence we appeal."

Refreshing to the soul after this exhausting week. It must have been at almost exactly the same time as you tell me you were singing it at home.

* C.C. nearly lost an arm through blood poisoning during his period of training for ambulance work.

Malo-les-Bains,
Dunkerque,
Sunday, 15th November, 1914.

I am constantly in the town now making purchases for the Adjutant, as our best French speaker has gone to the front, and I am understudy. Thus my off times have been reduced to a minimum, and though I have not had quite so much station work, I have been very busy. Shopping I thoroughly enjoy. The shop-keepers—men and girls alike —are most charming, and the English are evidently in good odour just at present. I have many pleasant chats, and sometimes drop into one or two of my best friends' shops to pass the time of day, even when I have nothing to buy.

I get into some awful muddles now that I essay rapid general conversation in French ; but it must be good practice. Both amongst civilians and soldiers (wounded and otherwise) I find very large opportunity for spreading Peace principles ; I tell them how I hate war. This is a new idea to most of them, except the mothers who have boys at the Front. They generally agree in word if not in fact. Of course one always assumes that this war must go on till a lasting settlement can be arrived at. To suggest other than that would hardly be playing the game to the authorities, who have enlarged the rigidity of the military machine to admit a band of peace lovers bent upon a mission of love. But one suggests that this may be the last war, if the right spirit prevails in human hearts. Particularly when one sees a group of soldiers gibing round a wounded German does one seem to be of some use in this direction. I tackle them something like this : " I don't reckon a man as an enemy any longer when he is wounded. It is not poor devils (*sic* : " *pauvres diables* ") like you and me and the wounded German yonder who make wars : it is the diplomats, the war lords, the rulers." They nearly always see the point.*

* Once a nurse who was helping me with the broken arm of a pleasant faced lad from Bayern added her German, only a little more ample than my own, to a distinctly interesting if scrappy chat about lasting peace.

The niggers are hopeless. Often they try to cut the
throats of German wounded—occasionally they have been
found with German heads in their haversacks ! Their
slow thought-out movements—such as in lighting a pipe,
for example—often suggests a monkey to me almost as
much as a man. And yet I am curiously fond of them.
Wag your head at them as you go by, and you win the
richest smile in the world, white teeth, thick lips, black
eyes, all combine in the most bewitching production.
They do not bear pain like the brave French boys. The
French authorities have been busy making the Shambles
very much cleaner and fitter for good medical work than
when we first arrived ; so, although the stream of wounded
never abates, things there are much more tolerable
now.

The town is of course cram full of army service motors,
provision lorries, etc., and soldiers everywhere. Of a
morning one sees a string of some forty huge motor lorries
off to the front with " *ravitaillements* ". The old two-horse
service carts which still work in addition, hark one back
to the Napoleonic Wars, and one meets the great ambulance waggons with tarpaulin hoods, painted dirty white
with huge red crosses—so familiar in pictures of the 1870.
The Turcos and Arabs, with their enormous baggy breeches
(in which they are said to carry the whole of their kit !)
are a wonderfully picturesque sight. The niggers carry
their kit on their heads.

It was jolly to see the new arrivals on Friday, and hear
a little news from England. They also relieve the pressure
of work at the Shambles. To-day I am off altogether
unless something unexpected turns up. Hence the muse
of scribes getteth busy within me. We had a very helpful
meeting this morning. I have had much in mind some
words of Van Dyke :

> " He that careth for the sick and wounded
>   Watcheth not alone ;
>   There are three in the darkness together
>   And the third is the Lord "

which led me very simply to a little service in the ministry.

I was given to understand yesterday that I should probably be required to go to the front to-day. But I watched the motor go off at 5 a.m., and had received no definite instructions. It took me all day to swallow down the resentful lump of disappointment that would keep rising. The advance party have a dressing station, from which they pick up the wounded from just behind the trenches. I had perhaps better not mention names of places, as I do not know whether the Censor would object. I should be glad to hear whether my letters are censored at all. I would not like to do anything that might be objected to. Our men are not actually allowed in the trenches. I understand it is the bandsmen who collect the wounded there, mostly at night,—many of the poor wounded, however, crawl out, and either fall on the way, or get to shelter under a wall or in a house near by. These our men get in and attend to. They say the suffering is much more frightful to witness at so early a moment. I dressed one poor old Breton *cultivateur* who had struggled all the way back from the lines with a great hole in his shoulder, which had never had any attention. Every garment on the upper part of his body (except overcoat) and to some extent on the lower, was a sodden mass of wet blood. You may guess how thankful I was to have a nice warm clean shirt to give him to put over the clean dressings (vide appeal in *The Friend*), of course all his original things I had to cut off and throw away. I expect I shall be going out to the lines very shortly : we only have a week there at a time, and then come back to the quieter work here. The dressing station is out of shell fire, but the collecting involves occasional exposure. It is the continual noise of cannon day and night that is said to be the chief strain. A Taube came over last Sunday dropping bombs, I watched it all the time—to-day I think it is too windy for a visit.

Advance Post,
24th November, 1914.
2 a.m.

. . . I wish I could tell you all about the work we are doing out here, but as I said on a postcard yesterday, we have received notice of a censorship on our letters of a very rigorous nature. However, I think I ought to try to send you a little picture of our surroundings, and trust to luck in connection with the blue pencil. The day, or rather night, when I first came out to the Front, will be ever memorable. Darkness, slashing November sleet in our faces, the little 'bus ploughing through seas of mud, out through Furnes to ———, where I have now been just a week. Progress very slow the whole forty kilometres, troops everywhere—" open fighting " is only just over,—regiments, batteries, constantly on the move. Every constriction—bridge, village, or the frequent zig-zag barrier of mud, with sentry demanding " *mot du jour* " meant a wait of half an hour or more. Guns galloped up, but mostly the steady tramp of infantry, both directions —mud-splashed men in long blue overcoats, red *kepi*, red trousers, and heavy kit, with the Frenchman's inevitable loaf, slung on the weary backs—silent from fatigue, but the cheery " *ça va ?* " always ready. (Airmen drop myriads of little steel arrows on bodies of infantry in the day-time, so movement is mostly at night.) Derelict motors lined the roadside, in the ditch, or shoved half way through a hedge—and dead horses, some flayed, ghastly sight as the headlight suddenly strikes them. Sometimes we had to tail dead slow for miles wedged into a huge convoy. We crept the last stages lights out. (" *Halte : éteignez vos phares : vous allez vous faire tirer dessus !* " screamed a French staff officer as he swept past in a Quartier Général car.) Shrapnel began to whine, guns were booming, tongues of flame spitting out all round in the darkness. . . . I am on a night watch at the moment, in a long upper room, dark save for the glimmer of the watchman's lantern carefully shaded against the direction of the German lines. All round are the sleeping-bags of the dozen or so who are manning this outpost. The flat country, studded with small villages, isolated farms, and wooded clumps, is snow-covered. All day long the guns have been thundering, they are quieter now, but still every now and then the silence is rent by three or four shocks in succession, which shake the house and make the windows rattle. The building is a convent school, run by a half-dozen of *religieuses*. The scholars are gone, but the nuns remain, absolutely fearless, and care for the wounded, mend and wash for the soldiers, etc. The Convent has been taken over as an overflow for the Evacuation Hospital posted in the village. In odd moments one goes into the nuns' kitchen to warm one's self at their ever cheerful stove. For four days the thermometer has stood at from 20 to 25° F. The nuns are angels. If one leaves handkerchiefs one has washed to dry on a shrub, perchance one finds that they have been taken away, ironed, and returned to their place—or one asks for a little hot water—such a rare luxury—and finds that a large potful has been kept on the stove all day " *exprès pour vous* ". Chairs always stand by the stove ready for when one comes in cold, and more often than not a basin of steaming broth appears. We live, move, have our being, sleep, wash (occasionally), cook, etc., etc., in the upper room aforesaid. Immediately below on straw lie wounded—too far gone to remove further—waiting for death. Around the large one-time schoolroom are ranged stretchers with the more hopeful cases—a smaller room adjoining is used for the " *salle de pansement* ". Next to me, when I turn in at the end of my watch, lies an English Tommy with a broken arm—stray ones come along and have the best time since they left England—but we have to pack them off next day to their headquarters—our work is with the French army. Our cars are out all day bringing in wounded from the extreme ambulance outposts, isolated farms just behind the trenches, for the most part, manned by a French doctor, an *infirmier*, and a few *brancardiers*—a soldier cyclist comes in with a note and off goes a car. In some of the villages near the lines there are larger dressing stations, and the cars go regularly and carry about fifty wounded a day from a single village.

Here, at the largest village of the neighbourhood, is a fair-sized Evacuation Hospital, as there is a rail or rather a tram-head. We take the most serious cases direct into Dunkerque in the fast cars. My work is a mixture of interpreter, car attendant and dresser.

Several old Sidcot* boys are out here, all of a younger generation than myself. I feel like a father or big brother to them—a feeling which waxes specially strong when they go out to the "*postes*" where there is danger, and I love to be with them. They are drivers, but excuse can generally be found for a car attendant, always useful in case of accident, to help lift stretchers, spout French, care for wounded (my little satchel of cigarettes and chocolates is always with me). In my heart I know that I go primarily as father, but it wouldn't do to let my boys know that! The other day I was going to Boesinghe with ———, who has only just left school. We saw shells falling on the village as we approached, but he drove quietly on, never even referring to them. I was proud of him! The ambulance "received" several shells whilst we were waiting there, and the French received orders to evacuate. We begged leave to "carry on", in the cellar if need be, and are arranging for a doctor and dresser or two to go down each day. The ambulance is in a convent, and we had to evacuate the nuns, one of whom was wounded. The road to B——— is very exposed : every farm damaged or burnt out, fields strewn with dead horses, often in heaps ; and just outside the village one of the wayside graveyards that one sees everywhere near the lines—forest of little wooden crosses, with the rude inscriptions of kind-hearted comrades : "*Mort pour la Patrie*", "*Mort sur le champ d'honneur*", or, with touching simplicity, "*Un soldat allemand*".

* A Quaker boarding school in the Mendip Hills, where C.C. was for several years a scholar.—ED.

I remained at the ambulance, to help load nuns, their goods and chattels—the car having to make a double trip. We had a long wait, and shelling recommenced, so I marshalled the company and we set off on foot. A " chattel " is a sheet tied together at the four corners, stuffed out to an enormous bundle. Each nun has two chattels. A nun would rather part with life than her chattel (Euclid !). The road came under fire as we proceeded, but the shells mostly passed over, spurting up mud in the field beyond. One burst in the ditch, however, and I got nearly frantic trying to speed up the convoy. When I urged abandoning the chattels, they simply sat down on their bundles in the middle of the *pavé*. Picture us : the stout rubicund dames streaming with perspiration, I ditto, for I was carrying chattels for the most toddly— and every now and then the uncanny whistle overhead. I got them ensconced in a dilapidated farm at last, roosting in silence round the kitchen floor—in fear for themselves now they had made sure of their things ! Mercifully, the car arrived soon after. . . . I think one has only a fortnight out here at a time. At Dunkerque the station work is much less heavy now, but our hospital needs a lot of orderly work to keep it going. It is mostly for medical cases, so there is not a great deal of dressing to be done there.

Hotel du Kursaal,
Dunkerque,
29th November, 1914.

Yesterday I crept at 5 a.m. in the pitch dark up to the little convent chapel. Mass at this hour every morning. The nuns had given me a warm invitation. Sisterhood assembled and half a dozen *brancardiers*. The intense earnestness of those kneeling men and women ! Rapture of a soldier's upward gaze as he receives the wafer on his tongue ! The intense silence—a crash, rattling all the altar tinsel, spattering the roof—crash—crash—not a quiver in those still kneeling forms, till the service quietly ends. . .

————'s car, standing at the gate, had its foot-board blown away ; he by the rear wheel at the time. . . . He seems to bear a charmed life !

I had an exceedingly busy day, which would appear more interesting if I could mention the places from which we were evacuating. " Evacuate " is the ambulance man's watchword, second only to " improvise "—the two together comprise his entire existence.

Had orders to return to Dunkerque for work at the new hospital, a charmingly situated villa on the sea front, with accommodation for fifty beds, of which some forty are occupied.

Arrived about 8.30 p.m. and got about one-and-a-half hours' sleep before going on duty at 12 midnight till 8 a.m.

Had an exceedingly busy time, as, apart from normal duties, I was constantly being called from one floor to another to interpret. I will write soon and describe the hospital work more fully. I am rather tired now.

> Hotel du Kursaal,
> Malo-les-Bains,
> Dunkerque,
> *2nd December, 1914.*

. . . I have just come off my fourth night's work at the hospital, and have not had time before to write about it.

I wish you could see the hospital ; you would feel that great work was being done if you could see the soldiers lying in their comfortable beds, cared for by the kind English nurses who have come out to help us—such a contrast from the rough beds of straw upon which they sometimes lie for days nearer the front.

Consider a man with a buttock torn off by a bit of a shell, who has been lying two or three days on a stretcher in a pool of urine, et cetera—such cases we get—or with a lump of jagged iron the size of a watch lodged in his neck, so that he can neither swallow nor speak—or with a bullet that has zig-zagged about in his brain and is still in it somewhere, shouting nonsense at the top of his voice for a week, and half of his body paralysed.

This man was on the straw out at ———— for three days, and I grieved to hear the *brancardiers* mocking—(" *se moquer de* ". I have translated the French, which came into my mind, literally—but the French word, with its sense of " making game of " expresses my meaning better), although his ravings were sometimes so funny that I could hardly repress a smile myself—one feels the tragedy even more when a lucid second or two comes, and he stops shrieking, "*j'ai soif! j'ai soif! j'ai soif!* "—and calls one and says quietly, " Ah, mon Dieu, if you only knew how thirsty I am." We have two such cases in one ward—they answer each other's ravings. The sooner they die the better. I was surprised to find the one from ———— at our hospital the first night I went there, as he had not been sent up by us, but had come through the ordinary channels of French evacuation. I have just been reading an article by a thoughtful, religiously-minded young man, who joined the army after the deepest thought, and from conscientious motives. His theme is that man has made such a mess of trying to run the world himself (materialism) that God has adopted this means of leading him to the only true way of running the world—" By my spirit ", and that therefore by fighting now we are hastening on the great day. My thoughts teem with refutations of such a theory, and I have hesitated whether to plunge into them (the refutations) in writing, and have decided not. All I will say more is that I hope all men who have fought and kept their conscience clean may be spared the sight of such as these—or their waking and sleeping thoughts might be haunted for the rest of their days by the horror, " I am the cause of that ". Personally, I would a thousand times rather be dead. There are several others almost as bad ; and at the Shambles I have in mind two cases that are even more hard to write of than these, and I will not try.

In some wards we have " *malades* ", bronchitis, malaria, pneumonia, pleurisy, as well as less serious ills.

All of these, mind you, are in the prime of life and heydey of their manhood—ought to be, I should say. The nurses (eight in number) strike me as being extremely clever and capable, and full of that supreme qualification of a nurse, selfless devotion to their work. Of course I have not a great deal to do with those at present on day duty, though I generally overlap them (as the night nurses do) by about an hour in the morning. One doctor lives at the hospital (I had to call the poor man up three times last night), and the others visit and operate during the day—one is always out at the front.

Our nurses have about half as many again the number of beds to look after that they would have in a large hospital at home ; hence each has a " nursing " orderly to assist her.

He does all the rougher work . . . preparing and serving meals in the wards, fetching and carrying, helping lift, and generally understudying. There is any amount to do. (The aeroplanes are a continuous interest—yesterday numbers of them were flying low over the sands like bugs before a storm—two have just passed my window, almost scraping the chimneys of the houses across the street—hence please excuse this little digression.) We are kept running about the whole time, especially I, who am in charge of the night shift. I allocate an orderly to each of the three night nurses, and am myself (as one would suspect of one so old and staid) entirely unattached ! I keep an eye on all, however, and help at the point where the pressure of work appears to be the greatest. There is one general orderly to do the rougher work of keeping hot water ready, fires and lamps alight, washing up, etc.

We have light refreshments about midnight and a half (as the French have it), and a rather more substantial meal about 4.30 a.m. with the nurses. But as someone usually has to be on watch in the wards, it is rather a straggling and broken repast. The French Tommy is a great man for writing letters and postcards home, which is—(another biplane right above the street)—

most excellent, but may have limits. I am told that a proportion of them (the missives) are deliberately " lost " in the French post—very hard-hearted of the P.M.G.* Some of the little notes to wives, sisters, daughters, cousins, that I have been privileged to read or write at dictation have been so touching as to make one feel inclined to weep. Praying them " not to have a sore heart " (literal translation of the French) on account of their wounds, etc. I feel this hospital is a great work, but it is also great to have its complement, the outpost—I hear we are to be entrusted with more work at the front—if so our turns for going out there will come round more quickly.

The hospital is no use for succouring the wounded unless someone goes out into the danger zone to bring them home, and it seems to me glorious to be able to do the whole work. Our fleet of motor cars grows daily, almost— I really don't know how many we have now, I have lost count. One is a wreck—the roads at the Front are awful —a carriage width of *pavé*—and on either side soft mud, up to the axle if one goes over—so that to pass anything is often attended with risk.

The motor drivers and mechanics, a large detachment, are as vital a part of the whole as any, and their work probably more fatiguing. I am going to have driving lessons ; not that I expect or wish to be a regular chauffeur, but to be able to carry on in case of emergency.

At the Front,
22nd December, 1914.

I have just received the two parcels you have sent me— —or rather, have just unpacked them. They have been waiting a day until I could find a spare moment. I am touched deeply as I think of all the kind thoughts which went into the planning of this lovely surprise, into the packing, and into the sending off, of the two noble parcels.

* A little external evidence for the impartial mind is the fact that one is frequently commissioned to obtain a dozen or even two dozen picture postcards for a single patient !

I wish you could see our contingent of nineteen men and
ten cars here to-night—if you could see us you would
realize very vividly all that your Christmas gifts mean to
us. All the glamour, if ever there were any ; all the
romance, if war *has* romance ; almost all the interest—
has worn off long ago. We are just grimly working out a
purpose. Wading about in thick mud, and through
incessant rain, from 6 or 6.30 a.m. until late at night.
Sometimes the uncertainty of war keeps us out all night.
It is mercilessly cold on the cars, everywhere. Sometimes
one gets a good night ; but I have not had my clothes off
for a fortnight. The soldiers march for ever backwards
and forwards as before. Reaction grips them too. *Elan*
becomes *ennui*. Unkempt, bedraggled, the troops move
to and from the trenches—pass in silence, without the
shout of cheer—with here and there a snatched embrace—
a sob—and "*si j'ai la bonheur de revenir*".   " No music now
or stirring drum, no banner proud," I haven't heard a
band since I came out, it's work is over once the boys are
on the troopship, glory fades into suffering.

When I last wrote I was at the front I think, since then
I have been down in Dunkerque in comparative peace and
quiet, but putting in strenuous work at the hospital—our
dear little hospital of . . . (censor) . . . beds.
My hands are so cold I can scarcely write. I am on night
duty for ten days. A large part of the nursing is being
done by males. I came to doubt whether the awful sights
and sounds of the firing zone were really the worst of all—
for I saw men come in smiling, bearing bravely their fearful
wounds, and then, despite the most loving care, day by
day, under the strain of continued pain, saw their nerves
giving way, and the strong faces of before were moaning
and crying—sometimes screaming throughout the night.
Of course, this was not so in every case, but it struck me
because unexpected. One thinks of it just the other way
round, as ——— pictures it in his article. He only paid
a short visit, and in the day-time, when a continuous
round of variety—visits, books, meals—helps to distract

the mind. In the long night watches, when sleep is denied by suffering, pain gnaws at the steadiest nerve. I have knelt by their bedsides, holding their hands, giving the drink incessantly demanded, doing the other little offices constantly needed, answering the repeated questions as to the time, speaking soothingly. Sometimes I have thought that the influence of a quiet personality with a pure purpose of love and goodwill to all men did seem to carry help and quietness, and one thought of another—a supreme Personality who went about long ago, healing—and of how much more one might do if one's purpose were purer, one's mind stronger for good.

Many of my friends I left in unrelieved suffering when I had to come away. In other cases, as I said, it was happily different. I picture one old man, apparently old, the first few nights he behaved so extraordinarily, throwing himself about in bed, making grimaces, jumping up suddenly, mumbling to himself that we thought he was mad —one night he tore his dressings off and started severe hæmorrhage, so that we found him lying in a pool of blood. When I left a few days later, he was quiet and sane, with a wan pathetic face and large eyes bent earnestly on one, telling us that the pain had been so awful he had longed for death—and at moments had tried to kill himself. For him, all that was over now thankfully. I think he would live, but I have not heard—how one longs to know about one's friends who disappear—we are here about as cut off from our people in Dunkerque as from those in England. Others one had just to make comfortable to die. I lost three of my patients—two were raving—with bullets in their brains, and screamed for twenty-three hours out of twenty-four ; for two or three seconds on one or two occasions they suddenly became sane, thanked one for a drink, spelled out their names for the register—one was swept by a great wave of hope, too soon to be blighted by the inevitable relapse, and as one thought of those moments of quiet, there came another wave of infinite sorrow at the thought of what might have been. The third died of typhoid ; we carried the bodies out to the little mortuary in the moonlight.

I loved the hospital work, but just as I was settling down to it, the call came to go out to the Front again. I think I shall be out for a long while now. At the . . . (censor) . . . we come into close touch with the doctors and field medical service—we are moving about with the constantly shifting army divisions, and the men who speak French are badly needed for the constant discussing of plans for work, arranging for fresh quarters, etc. ; also men with a certain knowledge of business to keep accounts, manage the stations, etc. Here we have an entire staff of paid chauffeurs, and with wages, allowances, buying of provisions, etc., the book-keeping becomes quite complicated. The demand is not so much now upon one's love and tenderness as upon one's power of administration. The poor wounded men pass through our hands in a continuous stream, unindividualized. But it is all part of a great useful work. One hopes that in the vast sheds of Dunkerque, there are now fewer men whose wounds reek with the awful stench of sepsis, than in the days (or rather nights) when we worked there—fewer stories of the poisonous gap of days, running sometimes into weeks—between trench and hospital—thanks in some small part to the efforts we make, the risks we take. And if the active, harder self, has to become prominent for the time in order that the needed work may be done, I am sure the gentler only waits its turn—ready. Indeed, I have just come from a tour of the wards, with our *Médecin-chef* ; we have been arranging Christmas trees ! And in part, your generous gifts have helped, as I am sure you would wish, to equip them with the loads that will bring joy to sufferers to-morrow. It is Christmas Eve. This poor epistle has suffered interminable delays, has lain on my desk in the middle of a sentence many a time. It must be very disjointed. But life itself is, at the moment, and a real letter should reflect it. One never knows when one may have to move on. A week—we may be 200 miles away.

All one's effects can be packed into one of our waggons—
and off we go. Turbulent days, these few before Christmas.
Dotted around here are our little outposts. A *grenier* here,
a stable there. On Sunday two of them were shelled
heavily, we got the news and off we went with four cars.
A deserted convent, in two corners of which our ambulances
were functioning, was largely in ruins. Half a dozen
brancardiers, our friends, lay dead. There was Dr. F——
and another surgeon amputating shattered limbs in the
" cave " (cellar), and the lads had carried down the patients
amid a tremendous bombardment. It was just grand,
and it seemed nothing less than a miracle that none of us
were touched. Standing amongst the ruins, I received
my first Christmas card this year, a French soldier gave it
me " from his sister ". A little pressed bunch of violets
tied with silk and mounted, with the words : " Remember
Germaine Périneau 16 ans Violets of France send by French
misses for the success of britannic, belge and french armies
—December 6th, 1914." Remember you, little Germaine ! Be sure I will. I dated a little word of thanks
from the ruins of Convent Sacré Cœur, asking her to pray
that peace might be restored. We could not complete
the evacuation that night. Dr. F—— and a few others
remained behind with their patients. I longed to stay
with them, but my duty was at our own place. All the
French ambulances had gone, not that they had any fear,
their duty was to go. Next morning we found a resting
place for the patients, and completed the evacuation, but
again the bombardment was heavy, and we found five
more bodies under the *débris*.

This outpost housed one of the homeless sections, so we
have been very crowded and busy. Dr. F—— and a
few helpers stay gloriously with a few old patients we dare
not move. No more shells have actually struck the
building.

Now I will write waiting for midnight mass. There is a
big church in this little country town (I am not quite sure
that Mr. Censor will think it quite suitable that you should

know that there are little country towns in this part of the world !), but an officer tells me it is not thought wise to hold the " *messe de minuit* " there, because the Germans might get news of so large a body of soldiers gathered together, and send bombs. St. Bertin already has buttresses and coping well scarred by them. So it is to be in the Chapel attached to this convent hospital. The Bishop of Nancy is coming, and a renowned Paris tenor is amongst our own *brancardiers* here, by the hand of the great leveller— War. All day long the clever hands of a posse of *Aumoniers* have been busy fixing up the *crèche*. It looks very jolly at the corner of the nave—a little gable backed by a rising slope, pine fledged and snow-sprinkled (did not *M. le Médecin-chef* wink as he initialled an unusually large requisition for cotton wool this morning ?), then inside, the Manger and Babe, Virgin and Magi, and Cherubs floating round. Really quite artistic. The loaves tomorrow all have little knobs upon them, and the baker says "*Le petit Jésu*", as you buy one. " Let us put from our minds all anxiety, all the sorrows and troubles of war " —the Bishop is speaking in a fine, clear voice, " Let us even put from our ears the noise of the cannon " . . . (how they have thundered incessantly all this Christmas Eve) " you soldiers desire victory, let us to-night desire above all things peace." Then comes a moment when in silent procession they file and kneel before the *crèche*, over which float the flags of the Allies.

We went over in our fast car this evening to ———, one of our little stations, seven kilometres away, to fetch the Union Jack, and ten of our head lights provided general illuminations, besides a battery of them picking out the *crèche* in brilliant white. Town gas supplies do not function in the fighting zone ! I knelt at the Manger, too, in spirit, and thought of Christ and the flags, and that perhaps He is nearer to the trenches than one thinks in one's moments of anguish at the horrors of war, nearer to the German trenches and nearer to our trenches. It is a clear, cold, starry, frosty night—a Christmas night (the fine day brought a Taube over us as usual). The tenor did not disappoint me. Particularly the duets were exquisite, and a violin. They marched out, and carried the Host around the wards. It is too late to go to my billet in a neighbouring street to-night—a small bedroom over a little stationer's shop, where I sleep on the floor—so I sit by the stove at our headquarters, and I think of all the dear ones at home this Christmas-time. My eyes grow heavy with sleep.

It is 2.30 a.m. on Christmas Day. Good-bye all my friends to whom this may come. Thought flashes you my love thus early on the morn of greeting—even before my pen can trace the words. Remember that I am supremely happy in this work that has been given to us, only grieving sometimes because with all the effort, all the expense, one touches such a tiny fringe. God grant that Peace come quickly—but till then, God grant us strength to go on, more and harder trials to bear. I find I have made my peroration, but I am moved to add an anti-climax. I need not have told you of the horrors of war—I ought to remind you of much that alleviates, or rather, helps us out here to keep sane and jolly. We have our jokes and fun—most things have humour somewhere about them. We fling away from anguish, and find ourselves laughing at things—it saves us. We scoured the country-side for a turkey. In a slack moment we sent out an ambulance to fetch him home, and he was carried in on a stretcher! Then we pooled our " plummers " and " mincers ", and if the Germans allow, we'll have our good old Christmas dinner this night, after all !

Thank you all for your contributions, a thousand times welcome. These unexpected packages from home have meant everything. . . . The building shakes with the roll of the thunder of guns, and I wish you all, dear ones, a happy Christmas, and close my eyes for a few hours sleep by the stove. At six all will be astir, and our work begin-ning for another day, so I will haste, and once again God be with you all.

21st January, 1915.

It is very difficult to find time to write at all, if one
remembers your injunction not to sit up late at night to do
it. I have had to sit up late several nights recently, and
didn't get any writing done, either ! On Friday evening
I was discussing with the Mayor of this little town (a
Belgian member of Parliament) the terrible spread of
. . . (censor) . . . and the steps being taken to
check it. To-day, Thursday evening, there are seventy
beds already installed in a chateau just outside the town,
English doctors, dispensers, nurses, orderlies ; English
blankets, medical stores, instruments, utensils. A garage
with two English ambulances and drivers, out daily
bringing in the patients. The old place lent itself wonderfully for a hospital, but the cleaning, carrying, arranging,
etc., that had to be done was a great labour. The bed-
steads, lovely little white painted cots, looking as dainty
as you please, all had to be brought from a hospital
(disused because of shell fire) eight miles away. Of course
with my regular French hospital and convoy work I have
not been able to do a great deal to help, but it pleases me
to think that I started the whole thing moving, and the
little I have managed has more than filled up the niches
of spare time remaining in an already busy day. Much
remains to be done—one hundred beds are spoken of.
The town simply reeks with disease. Each morning our
soup kitchen feeds crowds of refugees at the station—the
railway ticket being the soup ticket. The hospital here
(the large French military hospital where we live) is
crammed with wounded of the most serious nature. Fifty
came in this afternoon alone. I go round the wards when
I can, but have not been for several days, till a short visit
this afternoon. Only one hears the cries and groans
always, and cannot forget it is there. Last time I went
round I was shocked at the large number who had lost
their sight—so pitiful a lot—through balls in or about
the head. We are so fortunate with the men we have to
work with. Dear old Dr. . . . (censor) . . . of

Marseilles, our late *Médecin-chef*, was a fatherly old boy, with whom it was quite impossible to be on other than the best of terms. We used to dine with him and his staff occasionally, and were great friends with them all. They are at another hospital not far away now. L.J. and I ran over to see them the other day ; they fell on our necks as though we were long-lost sons. We are a little sad at losing our old friends. But see what happened ! Dr. ———— (Lieutenant-Colonel, rather a big gun) is perfectly charming and lovable, and as to his second in command, Dr.———— (*capitaine*), one can only say that if anything he is even more lovable than his chief. They are both amongst the most lovable personalities I have ever met, and it is a sheer pleasure to have to do with them. After the war, prepare to receive quite a stream of French officers *chez-nous !* I only wish some of them *would* turn up. One or two may. The invitations to stay at homes all over France which have fallen to me are legion. I watched our dear *Capitaine* a moment ago going round his beds (" *Mon cher* ", " *mon pauvre* ", " *mon petit* "). Then coming out of the ward he caught a glimpse of me, and came forward to shake hands. I think he knows that my heart yearns like his own kind heart for the poor suffering " *Pious-pious* ". There is so much that is at once painful and interesting. I sit at the open window of our " Bureau "—it is a clear night for once—the hour grows late. The sky all around is lighted up by the " *bombes éclairantes* " sent up to cast their lurid glare over the trenches ; the incessant thunder of the guns, and the sharp cracking fire of the rifles—the tongues of red shooting forth from our guns—the flash of white light of bursting shells. We seem so safe here ; this morning two enemy *aviatiks* came over, so low that we could see the black Maltese crosses underneath the wings—and dropped four bombs, but before that it was weeks since anything happened. And yet, one thinks, just that thin line of weary men in the trenches with their rifles, between us and the powerful enemy ever watchful to burst through at a moment of weakness or unguardedness.

But when I hear our guns booming, and the burst
of the shell after, " poor Germans," say I to myself in-
voluntarily, " I hope no one was hurt by that one," or
when I see them firing with rifles and shrapnel upon a
Taube, as they did this morning from our courtyard, I
shudder to see him brought down. I ought to be wild
with joy, you know ; but then I am a poor soldier, and a
special brand of patriot, it's admitted. One of the French
nurses who watched the firing expressed hopes of a very
different sequel,—" *Oh, si on pourrait le descendre !* " She
has brought a pistol in her kit, so I chaff her now when we
meet, saying I shall expect her to " *Descendre une Taube* "
with her " *revolveur !* " It is grand the way men give all—
their comfort, their lives, gladly to serve their country, in a
cause they believe to be right. But when I look out of my
window at night, as I do now, and see the bright starlit
sky prostituted by those blood-red patches of flame, I turn
away sick at heart, and go to bed and think that they with
all the sublimity of their sacrifice, are dupes ; we, dupes ;
all the world, dupes of the handfuls of charlatans who make
wars, exploiting, trading upon, those nobler traits of
human nature. " Your country needs you," cry armament
manufacturer, Junker, Chauvinist, well knowing that at
that cry millions of hearts that beat true and honest will
begin to beat proudly and courageously, and millions of
men will march out to slay their brothers. Thank God
from the bottom of my heart for the inestimable privilege
of being allowed to try to patch up the results of this
ghastly mistake. But oh ! the infinitesimal effect of the
patching. The awful smallness of one's self amidst these
vast forces. I was chatting to a lad in the wards this
afternoon ; both arms amputated, and he was trying to
compose a letter telling his *fiancée* about it. Another case,
in a bed near by, a young watchmaker from Besançon,
writing to break it to his father, whose sole support he is,
and whom he has never before left in his life, that he has
lost the sight of both eyes. A father arrived from Paris
this morning with the utmost speed of a pinched war-time

train service, to find his son buried a few hours before !
A Belgian mother in the town, with whom I have spoken
to-night ; no news of her husband for five months, and
still bright with hope ! A refugee who fled from Namur,
with three young children, now sheltered under this roof.
Her husband went into France to get work on the land to
support them; the Germans swept through and beyond the
village where he was working, and since then everything
is a blank—and the family of four lives on 4 frs. 50, which
the woman earns *per week* by working from morn till night.
Out of fifteen patients admitted to our new hospital here
during its first few days, more than half are dead. Aye,
and worse things than these one could tell, and this in the
tiny circle of one's own experience. But you could match
these instances with equally pitiful war stories from London
itself. One doesn't need to come to the battlefield to see
the results of the war. " When do you think it will end ? "
the Frenchmen ask me daily. I often think the moment
cannot long delay, when Humanity shall step in and say
" enough of this business "—that is if Humanity is still sane.

February 1st.—I see I began to write on January 21st.
Don't think I have been brooding over such gloomy
thoughts as those I see I closed with, in between—I've
been far too busy for that. I have a moment now after
lunch—we lunch at 12, and whenever possible I have to
be in attendance at a canteen which I have opened here
for my men, between 12.30 and 1 p.m., for sale of chocolate,
cigarettes, etc. It is greatly appreciated, and I am besieged
by an eager crowd most days. It is very difficult to get
supplies, and I have had to make two special trips to
Dunkerque for the purpose. To-day I have come back
rather early from lunch.
(At this point I was called off to interpret for Major
————, and spent the whole afternoon driving about
with him in his car—and both the men at the canteen,
and this letter, had to wait !)
Now I am waiting for the men to troop in.

4

February 8th.—Just another week gone, and no more written ; interesting events crowding in, and almost forgotten before one has time to write of them. This morning I mean to let everything go that can possibly be put off, and try to end this letter. Any directness, purpose, vigour, it may have had to start with must have been dissipated long ago ; and a poor emasculated sheet or two drag out a weary existence and limp in at last with the word " finis ". I almost think the *coup-de-grâce* had better be given at once. Much depends on the office door. The first tap that reveals a smiling be-galoned French officer seals the fate of this ill-omened epistle. I scribble a message of love—or leave that to be taken for granted— and sign.

I have left my billet in the town, and am now sleeping in the office. I found it rather awkward when we were called out at night, as occasionally happens, for a man to have to come out into the town, and wake the " *patron* " as well as us. I have got hold of a nice spring mattress, and a pretty blue blanket, and the whole looks quite chic, and the Geneva cross floating just above the pillow. My first visit to Dunkerque since coming out here on December 9th, was about a fortnight ago. I was almost as excited as if I had been going home. It was a good deal the same sort of experience ; here are the professional drivers, who are tremendously good fellows, but not quite the same as one's own friends. I drove a car in and back. I have been learning, though these roads are far from ideal for the purpose ; but I realized that knowledge of how to handle a car was of great importance, and decided to make it part of my equipment. Recently I have had enormous trouble with drivers being sick. We've had a sort of epidemic which has afflicted almost all, both here and at Dunkerque. I have had two on their backs on the average, for the past month—and have a regular dispensary ! So recently I have been doing quite a lot of driving. I think the greatest pleasure of the Dunkerque visit was going back to the hospital. Three of my old patients were still there and remembered me after all these weeks. One was obviously sinking slowly from shock, though his wounds were practically healed. The other two looked different men altogether—it was a great joy to see the improvement. They seemed very pleased to see me and have a little chat. Another great pleasure was being able to attend the English Church service. It was a Sunday—the whole of the rest of the time was spent making purchases for the hospital here (the French hospital where we live) and for various drivers. I landed at Church with a huge pile of parcels— but no one seemed to think it unusual !

I have all sorts of jobs to run in with my ordinary work. Translation into French of the Church of England leaflet of special prayers for war-time was entrusted to me by the nuns here. I thought it very broad-minded of them— they are getting it printed for distribution amongst the soldiers. I got my Belgian cook to do it into Flemish, too. The prayers are beautiful—nothing partisan about them. Speaking of the Belgian cook—he is a great source of anxiety. Personally I *like* the lad, and have promised to try to keep him. But the men hate him, and constantly I have to leave my work in the office to smooth out a terrific racket in the kitchen. Generally the root of the quarrel turns on an accusation that poor old Florent is poisoning the victuals ! It is really in part pure insular prejudice against the " foreigner", and of course in large part difference of language is the real trouble. Whatever the origin of the Babel story, no doubt the fact it dealt with has been a world scourge. I should be mighty sorry if there were no differences of language—the philologist in me would—but it is quite likely there would be no wars !

The time I was going to get for letter writing has been disturbed. For three and a half hours in bitter cold wind, I have been out with L.J. surveying for a water main from a stream to the hospital, where the well is exhausted. Surveying at night with lamps instead of poles is a novelty ! Now it is bed-time—so good-night !

I have just come back from a visit I pay every four days to a little girl whose leg was badly wounded during a bombardment. She is a refugee now in a cottage about three kilometres out of the town. A tiny stuffy room is crammed with some half-dozen men, half-dozen women, and four children. The temperature is astonishing, asepsis a thing to sigh for, and antisepsis operates under grave disadvantages. I dress the wounded leg—the crowd pressing round to watch the operation, awed into a breathless silence, broken only on one occasion, when I was stuffing gauze into the hole—a rather fearsome operation—by two single words, solemn and gravely uttered, impressive in the stillness : " ERMA ! "—" MARIA ! " Little sister's cry of sympathy ; big sister's grateful acknowledgment ! The child is rather sweet—would be quite in cleaner and purer surroundings. Last time she (Erma, my patient) gave me a little image in a box which she got at Lourdes (all the world here is Catholic, and the poorest of the poor scrape their pennies together to go to Lourdes—a sort of subscription scheme is opened, and a Cook's trip run in the summer). The way the towns bristle with convents and monasteries—Franciscan, Trapiste, Capuchin—is unequalled in any part of the Continent I am acquainted with. They are sort of " open " brethren and sisters, work amongst the people and all that, but one cannot help feeling that there are too many of them—too great a drag on the country. They are ever at work, but it is the sort of work of the historic villagers who lived by taking in each other's washing ! I believe every young girl, when she reaches the age of twelve or so, or say 75 per cent. of them, seriously consider the question of taking the veil. I know one or two who told me it was so in their own cases. Fortunately, they have been saved, probably by the instincts that makes them now such wonderful nurses. But to finish about Erma—to-night I found her making Valenciennes lace for me, throwing her bobbins about with the same rapidity and dexterity that astonished one in the Alpine valleys in far off, happier days.

I have had quite a lot of talk recently with folk about Quakerism, our principle against war, and of religion in general. I am surprised at the amount of sympathy and interest generally expressed. I found a doctor in this very hospital who said he could not fight for conscience' sake, but was satisfied to work in the " *Service de Santé* ". Two others would not agree that to fight in self-defence was against Christ's will—but while I was seeking to put the necessary quotation into French someone else did it for me ; the " other cheek " business, and one could see that it was a thought that had never struck them before, but which had come to stop.

I was delighted the other day to see how very kindly one of the nurses was treating a wounded German, and I asked her if she liked nursing them. The reply should be shouted over Europe. It will certainly remain for ever with fragrance in my mind. The pretty French shrug, and " *Il est blessé ; que voulez vous ?* " Our common humanity steps in and says that, amongst those who suffer, its spirit of love and kindliness must burst the limits of nationality, and break down the barriers of diplomacy. So let all of us in every land, in every clime, rise up, when mankind is sober again—all who suffer in mind, body, or estate (and that is three parts of the human race), and claim our right to this spirit of kindliness which *is* ; which we have a right to ; which we will never again allow those that make wars to filch from us for a single moment. The poor refugee woman I wrote about, who earns sevenpence ha'penny a day, has been ill for over a week. I can't think what will become of the three little ones. Take my word for it disease is more horrible than wounds. And people are all too busy to miss one figure about a place ; and too busy to occupy themselves with the matter if they did.

I have made one delightful acquaintance lately. It began by my noticing a small card pasted on a door in the town, announcing a Protestant " *culte* " for Sunday afternoons. Sunday afternoon is usually a busy time here, but

I have managed to go one and a half times, so far.   The Protestant *aumônier* (chaplain) is attached to a certain French army corps.   Each army corps has one Protestant, and of course numbers of Catholic *aumôniers*.   Before the war, and since the separation, there were no army chaplains at all, but the secularist army, if one may use the expression, seems to have broken down in face of the realities of war, and the *aumôniers* have been duly appointed.   Next Sunday, if the way open, I have promised to take the pastor out so far as one can go in a car, and walk on to the extreme *Poste-de Secour*, to hold a tiny Protestant *culte* amongst the small population—which consists of soldiers changing over —some going into, and others leaving the trenches, and of course the wounded who may not be in a position to profit much by the *culte*.   My *rôle* is to minister to the physical man with cigarettes and chocolates, whilst my friend busies himself with the spiritual.   It's always been my theory that the affair should be a pair harness one, and you see we are working it out even on the battlefield !

Monday,
8th March, 1915.

I am a little despondent at the moment—probably because a little overtired.   I have had to pull the accounts of the ——— Hospital here out of a horrible muddle. Thousands of francs spent, notes made on odds and ends of paper, no classification, no book save the *cahier* of a *gosse*, no one's fault, only three successive " *Comptables* " stricken down with fever in the act of formulating a scheme to put things on a satisfactory footing.   All this in my " *moments perdus*", *bien entendu*—and there weren't any of them, anyway !   So figures got into my head at nights, and I missed my sleep.   Now I am yawning—so with the office strewn with papers, and shape only beginning to emerge, I'm going to put work aside to-night, and give myself the pleasure of a chat with you—but mind, I'm a bit downcast, so you must discount my pessimism.   That's a preface.—

The management of this convoy now devolves almost entirely upon me, as L.J. has been busy putting in a gas engine, pump and about a kilometre of water pipe, to get a decent supply of water for the ———— Hospital. Now he is tackling another big installation job for them. I'm tackling their accounts, so we're quite proud of the way in which they come to us for their expert's work! But it all means long hours. I daresay the work that is being done at that ———— Hospital, with its splendid staff of doctors and nurses, would ensure the unit being mentioned in British army despatches, if the right folk got the credit at headquarters. At ———— on a certain memorable day in December, work that we did got some one else *cité* in French despatches. But the Quakers didn't come here to work for mead. However, I say as almost an outsider, that noble work is being done over there, where the four ugly towers of the " *Château du Juge* " stick up in the stormy March sunset sky. How the wind has roared to-day, rivalling the ever active guns—they've been specially busy too I believe, as though not to be outdone. You say I must be improving in French—yes, slowly, no doubt ; but always something unattained. It brings pleasure and pain too, this ability now coming to one to exchange one's deepest thoughts with others whose minds are cast in a mould so entirely different. That's partly too what makes me so sad to-night. " My husband's just killed two Boche officers," called out one of the *infirmiéres*, as we passed in the court just now. " *Tués chicment*," she added with glee, " I tell him that's not enough, I must have a dozen."— " Two will do for me," she added, after a moment's pause —" That makes fourteen the family ! "

I was in Switzerland when the war broke out. My often sadly obscured vision of God has lately hesitated much about interpreting any emotion as a " call ", but one lovely evening in August, as we wound down that exquisite bit of line from Fribourg to Lausanne, when the blue lake and distant glimpse of Mont Blanc suddenly appear, I stood out on the platform of the carriage, and it seemed

clear that I was to take up ambulance work at the front
if the way opened. For a fortnight my prisoner's mind
had been busy with the horror of the war that grew from
day to day, but this thought came into it then for the first
time, bringing peace ; to myself, only, alas ! The way
opened out unexpectedly, and during the weeks of preparation my purpose took shape in a phrase which was constantly in my mind : " To go out there so that there may
be one little *milieu* of love at any rate, amid the welter of
hate." I believe I have kept my end up from the
beginning. But to-night I'm to confess that it's often been
hard work. It is so difficult to explain one's-self—
especially in a foreign language. The other day I felt a
distinct " concern " to make a clean breast of my beliefs
to Colonel ———. He is a dear man, but constantly
he was accosting me in the street, anywhere, and beginning
his usual tirade against the Germans, insisting on his
determination that it must be a war of extermination.
Europe to be " *bien nettoyé* " of the *sales Boches*, once for all ;
and the Kaiser hawked round the capitals in a cage ! He
always asked for my confirmatory opinion so pointedly at
the end, that I thought he must have some object in accosting me thus. I usually blushed and stammered till he
came to the rescue by saying good-bye. So I went to
him one evening with my confession of faith, done in short
sentences of halting French, in my mind. He seemed
touched and kind. But I knew it was only a sort of affection
for the man, and not in any sense sympathy with the quaint
mind that rather amused him. Almost the same thing
happened with an English major, who seemed to take a
fancy to me, and whom I had helped a good deal as an
interpreter. There are others to whom I have spoken
with all the earnestness I can command—but the next time
I find the conversation has been forgotten, or is recalled
as a sort of *drôlerie* that couldn't be meant to be taken
seriously. You see this is quite the opposite of what I said
in my last letter. That's life. Two sides of it, and it's
best we should not hide the weaker one. One is such a

tiny atom and so helpless. It isn't that people aren't kind —English, French, all are—exceedingly. " I respect your views "—that is really noble, and more than one could expect in the circumstances—but you remain a phenomenon to be docketed and put aside on the shelf along with your beliefs. " You are *Utopiste*, very beautiful, but quite impossible," say the French. One wonders if, in some far-off time, when peace reigns, and the sound of cannon no longer rends the air, a word dropped here and there may be found to have borne fruit, after all ? And then, one is so often honestly in difficulty one's self, how to think. But all this is really no cause for discouragement, of course—except when one is tired. It is just because you may as well see me in a moment of weakness, that I allow myself to write to-night.

November and December were thrilling months for us out here. January and February have been almost monotonous—times rather of tremendous activity in useful if humdrum work. To rise regularly every morning at a fixed hour, albeit from a bed of rugs, to brush one's hair, even make one's toilet with some care, to have an office fire—all this seems far away from the dread realities of war. I sometimes like to think that the really best work I have done may lie in the quiet chats I have had upon the deeper things of life with one and another—but I have no proof—little hope of it. The Tommies—" *poilus* " I should say—I know have been glad to have me coming round their wards in moments spared from other work, sitting at the foot of their beds, but conversation becomes a little difficult even there when, as so often, the talk is of " *zigouiller* " the Germans. (You won't find that word in your Dictionary—it means killing with something of the *lust* of killing thrown in.) It becomes heartrending when they describe the circumstances in which they were wounded : " The Germans somehow got into a position to enfilade our trench, I was at the extreme end away from them—one by one we fell, like a row of ninepins—the man next to me remained after I had fallen, hit ; then he lay down—he pressed himself upon me to escape the bullets, one grazed his scalp, and the warm blood flowed over my face, the next moment he was done for ; it was 8 a.m. ; till 7.30 p.m., when it was dark enough to stir with some chance of safety, I lay perfectly still, my head and chest spattered all over with my comrade's brains. I was the only man who left the trench." One gets hardened to much. Only now and again the quick is exposed, and one quivers. . . .

One's outlook must be widened by such experiences ; by meeting with so many, so different from one's self, by getting once into the biggest stream of the whole world's history, and trying to keep afloat ! Once I stood by a " *soixante quinze* " that was firing on the enemy. The officer in charge invited me to pull the cord, and it was only the second impulse of thought that stayed the first impulse of interest and excitement. The horror of what I came near doing haunted me for days. And I haven't collected one single souvenir, from similar instincts (which probably sound overdone in this instance).—Not one, and do not intend to—save that touching one, the pressed flowers sent me by the little maid in far away Garonne ; and another, a present from the Christmas tree, when I took my turn with the wounded men in the wards ; and that from Lourdes I told you about. Every night this winter, from my bed, I have watched before going to sleep, those uncanny glares over the trenches. Attacks have been made, perhaps more than you at home guess. Counter attacks. Results have hung in the balance ; but the volcano upon the edge of which we have been dwelling has remained quiescent. It will not continue so for ever. More precious life must be poured out. Within a few miles of here, a few months ago, half a million men laid down their lives in two or three days' fighting. How gladly one would show the " greater love " if it were required. What a glorious thought that God has huge tasks, infinite difficulties to be overcome, dangers to be faced—elsewhere, for those whom He has watched here tackling jobs, and found trustworthy. I don't think we need worry about our fighting instincts suffering if we refuse to use carnal weapons. Be sure there's nobler fighting to be done somewhere else, even if not here. Some of us think there's plenty here yet (social conditions, for instance), but anyway, if not, it's a quiet moment of preparation, just as the army corps continually move backwards and forwards between the trenches and the villages of " *repos* " well behind the lines. And if we prepare well, or fight well, it's going to be a promotion when we move on !

So we don't know what lies before us this spring and summer, but we try to prepare. Perhaps it may all be over suddenly, soon. As I go about in the khaki I'm proud of, amongst the soldiers, I believe that the man who saw that first boatload of English troops landing at ———, and moving off to the front, and forced back the scalding tears at the horror of it all, is a stronger, braver man, and not less a true and tender one, for all that he has lived through since then. Now I must say good-night.

Sunday, March 21st, 8.30 p.m.—Calculate how long it is since I began this letter ! Since writing that first instalment I have not had a moment in which to continue ! Eh, but it's grand to have heaps of work to do, when it's all helping where there is so vast a need. I am again very tired— but in good spirits this time. " *Remontez votre esprit !* " I say to my dear *blessés*—which is, being interpreted, " cheer up ! " as nearly as I can do our fine English phrase into my (doubtful) French.

It is extraordinary how one's state of mind at the time of writing a letter influences what one says. I often wonder whether other folk are so impressionable as I am in this respect, it doesn't seem a good thing. However, to-day, in spite of a bad headache, and an order to go over to the *Quartier-Général* of the —th French Army on business, fifteen kilometres away, just as I had finished a long day's work, and was on the point of lying down for a short rest with " Palgrave "—in spite of that, I am in excellent spirits,

and very fit. I never cease to be thankful for the extraordinarily good health I have had. I try to keep myself
fit—the constant inspiration of this work makes all such
efforts easy. You will understand that I am anxious to
put in every moment available at my work. One might
so easily be cut off from further service at any time, that
one longs to do the utmost while health and strength are
his. I feel that I have lived my life for this—to be just here
just now ; and if I were required to give my life there
would seem a certain completeness about one's small
efforts after righteousness. But one ought not to think
of that. I'm sure it won't happen because I sort of feel
I've so much to do yet. The joy of it is wonderful amongst
all the sadness. And do you know, I sometimes feel as
though I were on the brink of converting all this Hospital
staff to Quakerism. There is my sanguine moment,
voyez-vous. Let it cancel out what I said in Chapter I,
and arrive yourself at the sane estimate of my actual
position. Whether I am considered a harmless maniac or
not, no doubt that I get on well with the doctors. Can you
imagine me passing the psychological boundary which
separates folks one *handles* from more distant acquaintances ?
This is what I mean—can you picture me walking arm-in-
arm with, standing with both arms outstretched, hands on
the shoulders of, etc., etc., men, some of whom are amongst
the most eminent surgeons in France ? Yesterday afternoon
a great honour was paid me—a doctor came running up
to my office, asking me to join a group of staff and doctors
of the hospital which was about to be photographed !
And there, blushing and spluttering questionable French,
I was pushed bang into the middle immediately behind the
dear old Colonel himself. Just as things were ready a
Taube came over, and *M. le photographe* disappeared !
A long search all over the huge building and grounds
ensued, before the young man could be found again !
It's simply impossible to tell you all that happens. One
day—the dear day when Peace reigns again—we'll talk
it all over. So much crams itself into such a short time.

Each few days that slip away without a word from me, there sinks in temporary oblivion something I should wish to speak to you of. Temporary, because I am sure that in the days to come chance allusions will call back this and that which one will be glad to remember. There are the wounded always—how terrible to see I can never let you know ; and worse still to know that these hundred or so beds here with their loads of misery, now discharged by death, now to be dragged through an aimless existence of years (rarely otherwise, for this place is for very serious cases only) are not an isolated set of facts—they are types of thousands and thousands in half the towns of Europe— and worse yet, it is a *stream*. That came over me with fresh horror only the other day. Several times a week I go round the wards—always new suffering faces and forms. One has only to live here a short while to have an awful fact forced on one. Of the great stream that flows continually in, there is a backwater, a considerable one, that flows no further, except yon short journey headed by the *prêtre-infirmier*, with white surplice over his astonishing red breeches, head down murmuring from his prayer-book, and behind, the *cerceuil* on the soldiers' shoulders, and the tricolour over it, and we saluting by the roadside—every morning. And one notes the thinner stream that floats on beyond our ken. And yet I dare to say there is little one will not be glad to remember ! Because one is here to follow the example of One that was amongst men as him that serveth. I am struck daily by the amount of love about. Here to-day is a lovely spring twilight after the brilliant round of the sun, and every one who is free strolling about under the brightening crescent moon and glittering stars and crimson west sky, and every one, French, English, Belgian, greeting every one else, because every one feels the need of being friendly and loving to some one. So Tommy calls out " *Bon Soir* " to *Piou-piou*, and " good-night " calls out the latter, and " *Goeden dag* " or " *Tot wederziens* " they cry in chorus ; for, French or English, a soldier boy must learn his few Flemish phrases, you know, or how could he crack his joke with the fair Flamandes ? One looks around, with the gloaming the *bombes éclairantes* are beginning to flash white, and the little pouf-poufs that have been all over the background all day are beginning to be preceded by spots of flame as the blue deepens into black, and the aeroplanes make off to the safety of their own lines with the fall of night. So one cannot escape the fact that there is war, even on this beautiful Sabbath eve—but everyone seems kind, and to feel that the other business is just a hateful necessity that's got to be gone through with. Last Sunday night the noise of the guns was positively *épouvantable*—I don't know any English word that seems to do so well. I had taken one of the French doctors to our English vespers—an avowed atheist, and he was deeply impressed. Not that he understood much, it was the fact of this roomful of English soldiers, so evidently devout, and the fine young chaplain so evidently in earnest—(how could the English, a nation so "*pratique*", believe in anything that was all moonshine ?) and " You'll end by converting me," said my good friend, Dr. ———, who's a Christian already although he won't admit it, because his life rings pure and true and gentle. After that I dined with the doctors, and a terrific discussion ensued touching the advisability of setting aside a company of the probable geniuses of the rising generation, and exempting them from the trenches. The noise, heat and champagne made it difficult for me to keep my head, it was a bad start for a night's sleep, anyway. There followed the most awful din I have ever heard in my life. After an hour's ineffectual effort to sleep, I rose, and sat at my window in an overcoat till 5 a.m., when the first mass bells began to sound, and the racket died ; all night long I watched our guns flashing and the German shells bursting, listened to the whistle of the shot through the air, the softened thud at the other end, or when a great shell was coming this way, one heard nothing until the very earth seemed to shake with the concussion—and the whole horizon was one continuous blaze of light. An attack was being made on our lines, of which you will since have read in the papers, but you may not have known that it was so near us.

Tuesday, p.m.

On Saturday I had a great treat. Some doctors had to go up to Dunkerque on business, and others availed themselves of the opportunity of going for a day's excursion. " Tell Catchpool to come too if he can get away, and lunch with us at the Chapeau Rouge "—so the Doctor delivered the message entrusted to him by his colleagues. Incidentally I direly needed a bath, and managed to get away. I did my eight friends the honour of driving them up myself, and then I took Dr. ———, our chief surgeon, and another doctor out to an immense hospital on the seashore some ten kilometres out from Dunkerque (if you remember a huge building we saw on one happy occasion steaming close in on a voyage from Ostend to Dover, it is the very place !), there are 2,000 beds, and perfectly wonderful equipment. Every bed can be raised off the ground by a lever, which at the same time lowers a pair of rubber tyred wheels and allows the whole to be wheeled with ease into the operating room. I saw several operations. My companion was Dr. ——— of Nice, I had to refuse his genial invitation to lunch, as I had to go to the dentist and also visit our *Quartier-Général.* I've lost two good molars since the war, and miss them sadly ; " *Das ist Krieg* ", murmured I, as out they came, well knowing that they would have been " capped ", " plombed ", or otherwise " conserved " in times of peace. My goodness, what a tiny loss ! Issuing from the dentist's, I met Lieut.-Col. ———, a dear old friend who left here last December, and whom I thought to be at another part of the front five hundred kilometres away. I had an even more serious difficulty in refusing a second invitation to lunch at the " Taverne Charles ", and mind you, all these high officers, who are so kind to me, are professional soldiers. Everything above a First Lieutenant is ; it astonishes me abundantly that they should

have anything to do with a Quaker who does not hide
his views. "*Il y a beaucoup de monde en Angleterre qui me
feraient volontiers fusillé pour ce que je viens de vous dire,*" I tell
them, but it doesn't seem to affect their friendship. It is
the inherent love in human nature coming out in spite
of itself. Be sure I don't forget to add that there are many
in the old land who think as I do too. It has been an
inspiration to me in my work out here to read in *The Friend*,
and in the letters from all the dear home folk, of the wonderful work you are doing for Peace. I felt from the very first
that we had work to do both at the front and there—that
it was all part of the same work—how unworthy I felt of
being amongst those that went out, what a privilege it was !
But the work at home is absolutely as important, and more
praiseworthy, because less interesting. . . . The
Monday after that eventful Sunday evening I attended a
wonderfully impressive funeral service on the victims of a
bomb raid. Our poor little town suffered heavily—
eleven coffins were in the aisle, some with the bright
national flags, some with the black civilian pall. Seven
died in our hospital the night before, and I watched to the
end with one of them, a poor fellow sucking air into his
lungs at every breath through a great hole in his
chest. . . .

. . . In the evening I had dinner with the staff of
seventeen doctors at another hospital in the town. You'll
think I spend all my time drinking champagne. No !
it's mostly pretty solid hard work—these little sparklings
on the surface are rare as the wine. Captain ———, of the
English clearing hospital, was also a guest this evening ;
I often go in to chat with him, and his chief, Colonel ———.
It has been one of the great surprises, as one of the greatest
pleasures, to find how warmly the English have welcomed
and appreciated our work. I was introduced to an English
General the other day. They put more work on to our
shoulders almost than can be managed. This is the work
you read about in *The Friend*. The work of our convoy is
entirely for the French, and does not get mentioned—

our cars form a definite part of the *service de santé* of the
———th French army—we are "*poilus*", if you like to
put it so, whilst retaining full liberty as volunteers. In a
few days we shall commence feeding with the French (we
have fed ourselves up to the present). I tell my men I
shall have a good laugh at them then ! We are living on
the fat of the land, I am often ashamed to think how well ;
it is wartime and yet there are often complaints—I guess
there will be more when we subsist on French diet !

It is nearly an hour since I wrote the last word—things
will happen, just when one has hopes of actually concluding
a letter ! I have " come from assisting at " another bomb
raid, the second within a few days. Suddenly I heard the
anti-aircraft guns (little town so near the lines would feel
it *infra-dig.* to have a siren !) I laid down my pen, stepped
across the courtyard where the cars are ranked, started up
the " Deasy " and ambled towards the Grand Place,
" looking for trouble "—I know that as officer of the convoy
I ought to go and rout up some of our professional drivers—
a dozen of them lie snoozing or smoking or reading on the
straw at their quarters, next door to the office. Well, but
they "grouse", whoever one happens to pick, it isn't his
turn, or he's not well, or his car not ready, for some un-
exceptionable reason—then, it is mighty slow work getting
him under weigh—all which time your adjutant is itching
to be off himself ! So he starts up the " Deasy " (because
it's got a low " bottom "—13 to 1—I believe, a very present
help in trouble), and rolls gently towards the Grand Place,
one eye cocked aloft. From the Grand Place roads radiate
through the town, and one can generally pick up the trail.
I stopped at the corner. There he was, very high, little
black speck in the dull grey. " *A-t-il lancé des bombes ?* "
" *Non, mais il a l'air.*" You may well be laconic, *mon cher.*
Hardly were the words out of his mouth when a great cloud
of dust rose 150 yards down the Rue ———. Simultane-
ous series of crashes. The engine had been turning over
quietly all the time, so I was in the dust cloud in a matter of
seconds. Before I had stopped, some R.A.M.C. men

were pulling stretchers out behind—struck me as very
smart. If they had thought about it at all, they must have
concluded I'd dropped from the sky with the bombs, sort
of providential counter-dispensation ! but at the front one
just takes things as a matter of course. Here were
R.A.M.C. men off duty, sauntering along the street—
bombs, wounded, ambulance, stretchers—all very natural
and in order, and the men at their work before they have
time to think ! I caught sight of a little Frenchman I knew
and shouted " run like hell to Ambulance Anglaise " (I
forget the French phrase I hit on, but I know it was
strong—)" tell Sergt. to send me four cars at once, Rue
———— "—he was off like an arrow. Three great dray
horses lay in a disembowelled heap at top of the camber,
blood flowing into the gutters—footpaths littered with
prostrate forms, houses gaping on either side ; but they
were already lifting stretchers into the car—an English
Major and a Captain one side, wounded—two Tommies
on the other—poor beggars, no better than little heaps
dumped on to the middle of the stretchers—baskets
would have done better. Those R.A.M.C. men not quite
so wide awake as I thought, taking me for a hearse !
Dead slow through a few narrow streets to the clearing
station, crowd waiting at the door, several doctors from
our French hospital over the way amongst them. Before
I left again two more of our cars had tailed up behind and
were discharging—quick work (the men shall have praise
when due)—that made twelve into hospital in about as
many minutes ! I fetched a circuit and approached for a
second load from the opposite side, but was blocked by
débris whilst yet afar off—asked someone how many
casualties ; was told nineteen, and in the distance saw
our fourth and fifth cars loading. As I was turning in
the road way, a man I had never seen before called out
" Good old F.A.U. ! " We had sent out twenty stretchers
in all, so I was free to make for home and my letter of
which I now resume the thread, after this little episode
in an *ambulancier's* life. . . . Poor little town badly hit

again, and it's only a week since we buried the last victims. My men have been naming their cars—mostly the names of wives or sweethearts, *ça va sans dire*—I have called mine " Frank Crossley ", it is a lovely car by the famous Manchester firm whose founder's life is such an inspiration to all who hunger and thirst after righteousness. I have taken much pleasure in painting on the name my very best, and I like to think of this car, carrying on, in a sense, the work that was started in the old Star Music Hall at Ancoats —a work of helping the suffering. The struggle in which the men he helped had gone under and suffered was different, but if love had more perfect sway both wars would cease. This awful conflict—the more obvious and tangible, will end before its subtler shadow. Perhaps I do wrong to press comparisons too far, but we do not lay down arms till love is supreme everywhere—and then as I said before, we're promoted to a bigger job still elsewhere. Don't think I'm getting military—proud of having to do with high officers, etc. Do you know, until the present war I could hardly think of a soldier as a human being ? They were something so apart from me that I could not even bring myself to cry " good luck " to those lads going off from ———— in August—(perhaps that was something to do with the lump in my throat though). Anyway, I'm certain I'm a saner man to-day than I was before I had to do with soldiers. They are just dear human souls, pretty simple mostly, lovable and the very salt of the earth for kindness. I haven't seen them at a bayonet charge—I may do yet—but of this I'm certain, that the souls lag behind those charging bodies ; it isn't the souls we know and love that do it—it's the devils that you and I are responsible for having left prowling about on the earth. And when they come back bleeding, and it's all over, that frenzy—they're so still and gentle and loving again. How I go yarning on ! It's more than time I was abed. I shall steep a few *feuilles de tilleuls* in hot water in a moment—the kind *infirmières* heard I hadn't been sleeping well, and sent me up a *tisane*—it has wonderful effect, and I have no fear of not going to sleep now, and I wake up as fresh as a lark. Apropos *infirmières*, my tours of the wards with good things, which began before Christmas, have resulted several times more recently in a pleasant chat and a cup of tea in the nurses' room afterwards. I confess to looking forward to this, and at the same time to a feeling that my visits to the *salles* are not so entirely disinterested and creditable as they once were ! My French has even risen to the demands of a very mild and honest flirtation, but alas ! in ten days the " *Parc* " of *infirmières* has to go, by special order of the General commanding the ————th army, who will have no more women in the immediate zone of hostilities. I am " *navré* " (which only means " sorry " in spite of what the dictionary may say) and shall miss them. Further, I can't imagine how the hospital will get on without them. By the way, I had a very high honour paid me a little while ago. My chief, the Hon. Lionel Holland, came down from Dunkerque to make an inspection of this convoy—he was introduced to Col. ———— (the French officer whom I work under) " who commands the convoy "—" Pardon," was the reply from the Colonel, " It is our dear colleague, M. Catchpool, who commands." Well, after such vociferous and unpardonable blowing of my own trumpet, I will to my " *tisane* " and bed.

SECOND BATTLE OF YPRES

I HAVE just found my first moment of calm for eight days. Just eight days ago this awful battle began, and now there is a lull, and I am sleeping back in the old town, my residence for five months, to get a real good rest. The affair is not over yet. Our little group of ten cars flashed up to forty from various points of Belgium and Northern France for the emergency—we are holding them together, and thoughts of more than momentary repose cannot be entertained. It is about six o'clock in the afternoon, and I am sitting alone by the brook, at the end of the College garden. This great *Collège St. Stanislas*, which rang with the voices of 400 boys, until war filched from them the priceless benefits of education ; that echoed all the long months of a wet winter to the feet of the *brancardiers*, that hummed with the swarm of R.A.M.C. orderlies, who hived a great English clearing station here for a few brief weeks. This great college is deserted and silent as the grave. The doors are locked, no one can enter ; only I am privileged, for the principal priest, my friend, before he fled, left me a key. One does not live under a roof five months without accumulating a good deal of *débris* of one kind and another, largely worthless, perhaps, but the best of mortals is enchained a little by his " things ". So I have not conveniently been able to move entirely to an estaminet a quarter of a mile out of the town, where we presently live, move and have our being ; and as the Principal has given me the run of the place, I retire to my old office from time to time for a moment's quiet work, which is impossible yonder, where a personnel of sixty crowd the tiny rooms of a wayside bar ! So I creep into the vast building, silent and alone, like a mouse prying into a large kitchen of nights, when cook has gone to bed. I have been at work in the office all the afternoon, and now, as evening draws on, I have taken a chair to the brook that runs at the bottom of the garden. Till seven I am free ; then supper, and after that bed, I guess. So I dedicate part of my first moment of repose for eight days to you. For nine days and nights now I have not had so much as jacket, boots, or leggings off —for five I hardly slept at all, and now I feel that I could do so for a solid four and twenty hours. Only this evening of peace and quiet after the awful turmoil, the bodily fatigue, the mental pain, of the past days, is infinitely sweet to me. In the field across the brook a group of Indians squat on the earth around their camp fire, and prepare an evening meal, chattering to each other in some oriental tongue. Wonderfully picturesque they are, in their khaki puttees and knickers, loose flowing khaki jackets and wonderful khaki turbans, the whole blending so well with their dark brown skins. They are tall, handsome fellows with fine eyes and lovely white teeth. The majority are bearded, they stand up straight as an arrow, graceful, flexible. If one greets them as one passes in the street, the richest smile in the world is one's reward. How kindly and genial they are, these children of the East ! One would not think of smiling a greeting to folk one passed in the streets of London or Paris—or if one did, one's answer would be a stare which enquired—are you mad ? But with these simpler people one's little effort at friendliness never fails of its reward. It is just the same with the Senegalese. Has our Western civilization been an unmixed blessing ? Certainly we have gained much, but I am sure we have lost something.

This stream swarms with rats, they keep hopping out of the dirty water, and scampering along the bank so close that they almost have to jump over my boots. They are not creatures I am fond of, but I do not feel any enmity towards them this evening, because everything is so peaceful. The guns are at last still—how thankful one is for a moment's pause from that noise that is a thousandfold more terrible than mere *degree*, because of *kind*. The garden behind me is white and pink with spring blossom. The trees are green and the lawn also, save where the patches of brown denote the positions of the half-dozen R.A.M.C. tents lately there. The town is deserted and absolutely still. It has been a lovely day and now the sun is setting behind the empty College. I have been wandering through the maze of rooms, and found two cages of birds in the nuns' kitchen—two little green parroquets, and a dove. They might have carried the little creatures off with them when they fled so precipitately (in one of our cars !) to St. Omer and not left them to die of starvation. I carried the cages out into the garden and left the doors open—it was all I could do.

The Indians are baking " chapaties " upon their fire. They take a lump of dough, flatten it in their hands, passing it over from one palm to another, patting away till it is flat and round and smooth, then they lay it on an iron plate raised a little on bricks, and poke bits of burning wood underneath—all the time they talk, but never lose their dignity and stateliness. The guns still wait—I cannot express to you my thankfulness for even this moment's sense of peace.

On Thursday evening, just over a week ago, I was at the little village where we were to be quartered with a large French ambulance at the " *Petit Château* ". A torrent of cannonading suddenly commenced. We sniffed the air, and on the north-east wind came floating down the attenuated odour of nauseating fumes. And from an upper window I saw dense clouds rolling over the trenches. We had business in P———, and our route lay by way of a ruined city, whose fallen stones had afresh for days been battered by the tremendous German siege guns. Over the ill-starred place hovered a dark brood of Taubes—war vultures gloating upon their carrion—gliding about low, regardless of the shrapnel that burst all around them. The road home seemed to be the earth-trail of another brood, speeding back in single file to the German lines. With eyes fascinated by the spectacle, I saw a shell burst upon one of them, and almost immediately a body of flame descend. A cheer broke from a group of Tommies by the roadside. They thought, as I did, that he was hit, his petrol tank alight, but no ! To the right and left others had branched off, and dropped simultaneously their balls of fire. Thinking geometrically, one realized with a shudder that the villages were being marked out for German gun practice. It was sinister, that pungent smell, that tornado of guns, the arranging of those village targets. We made a hasty meal. Our duty was at the front, and even as we ate there came the tramp of running feet, the cries of hoarse voices shouting, " The Germans have broken through, every man that can carry a rifle come along ! "

Away we went to the ambulance at ——— with all speed, past the reserve trenches, fully manned. The wounded— nay, the poor choking, gasping, dying, asphyxiated beggars were already beginning to pour in. We could do nothing but transport them with the utmost speed to safety and proper attention. All through the night our 'buses beat it back and forth to the rail head, eight kilometres away, with their ghastly loads, and we made hot drinks on our Primus stoves for those who were not insensible. That night the Germans were across the canal, within one and a half miles of our ambulance, which stood unprotected in the middle of a great rent. Had the Germans realized it, we should surely have been at least prisoners to-day. The battle raged five days and five nights before it began to abate. We had the soup kitchen sent down, and every second of the twenty-four hours we were serving out hot Oxo and cocoa, biscuits and chocolate. Periodically they shelled the village. We ran the gauntlet until one driver was wounded and two cars put *hors de combat* ; then we made a detour. The detour became unsafe, and we had a red flag signal from an upper window, seen from afar, warning the drivers that shelling was in progress. The wounded followed the asphyxiated. Blood covered the stretchers, dripped from bandages upon coat and breeches, lay in little pools about the drive and steps and flower-beds.

Still we worked, and flung ourselves down now and again for a brief sleep. Then they began to shell the rail-head too—small ones for two days. We had to run up with each load of wounded. The sinister scream and bang, somewhere about the poor little town, one after another, and one wondered just where the next one was going to pitch. A breathless messenger comes for cars, and we go out with two, to behold, perhaps, one of the most pitiable spectacles the war will disclose—a whole ward of the civil hospital wiped out ; eleven corpses, mostly nuns (the *infirmières*) strew the floor, the dust of plaster whitening them, choking up the streams of blood, and an old *père Trapiste*, with wounded head, tottering about, helping everyone, playing the hero, amongst it all. Out again to the front, where men, filing up from the reserves, passed the ambulance gates gay and singing, to be carried back to us, maimed, upon stretchers, within an hour. The roar of hundreds of guns, before, behind, on both sides of us, was continuous and appalling : almost terrifying at times. At night we were creeping silently out to the *postes de secours* just behind the trenches, with our smaller cars, where the shells crashed startlingly, and the *bombes eclairantes* threw up black shadows like moonlight, drawing the bullets, what time one lay prone in comparative safety till it was over. The lanes were blocked by piles of earth thrown up by shells exploding in the ditch, or pits dug by them bursting on the *pavé*. One dodged the holes and tore away the earth with hands and feet, and bumped on bottom gear over the *débris*, to the accompaniment of groans within. Fires raged everywhere, glaring in the sky at night. Soldiers lined the hedges. Dusty men, wounded, tired-out men, straggled and tottered back from the lines. Barbed wire sprang up everywhere. Regiments wandered about lost. Meadows suddenly became packed with horses ; villages swarmed with troops, guns, material ; then suddenly emptied, because something had happened, and one realized the purpose of those sinister fireballs. Under the hot sun by day, the growing moon by night, the soldiers marched up, dusty, tired. Canadians, Tommies, Zouaves, *Poilus*—all filing silently across the fields, dustily along the roads, towards the hell that raged ahead, asking one, in a whisper, how far it was to the trenches, from which probably they would never return. It *was* hell. That was the word on everyone's lips, in one's own mind.

We went to the *refuges des blessés* that lined the south bank of the canal that will be for ever famous.

Dead horses pulled one up short, lying right across the road. I remember, too, a little dead calf in one place too small to bother about, the wheels had got used to going over him. Passing an aid post with an over-loaded car on one occasion an orderly rushed out, saying : " For God's sake, stop ; I have not had a car for two hours ! " and behind, stretched on the plain in the moonlight were 400 wounded Canadians.

Then they started shelling the ambulance itself. The garden was pocked with holes, the room we live in strewn with *débris*, the kitchen car was riddled, but we went on working, no vital part being touched except the Oxo boiler, which was holed, and which we could only half fill now. We moved a few hundred yards back into some sheds. Still they shelled us ; but up to the present we have not been touched. The fields around are fairly pitted, though, and I have slept out there under the moon the last three nights !

A considerable number of German wounded came into the ambulance one night. I talked to them, one I asked about the supply of provisions in his native land (after tasting a bit of his " *Kriegsbrot* ", which I found not at all bad). He said he had been away from home so many months without news that he had no idea of the state of things. Another elderly man attracted my attention by his pleasant pensive face ; I told him that I was sick and tired of the war. " I think we are all tired of it," was his reply with a wistful smile. As I handed a cigarette to another he shot me a look of surprise, and cried to his companion, " See, the English do not hate us ". " Do you hate the English ? " we asked. " No, I think the Kaiser and the King and the Czar ought to fight out their quarrels by themselves, and leave us poor men alone." The French doctors and *brancardiers* were kind to them, poor, terribly mangled human suffering bodies, all the hate gone out if it were ever really there—who could help loving, at least, pitying them ? I was up at the rail head when the first terrific explosion occurred on Monday afternoon. I thought the old College itself was hit, the whole building and courtyard were strewn with dust and *débris*, and a piece of hot, mangled iron flung to our door.

We ran from room to room, and out into the garden fearing every moment to come suddenly upon comrades lying dead. The shell had not struck us. We took our car and stretchers for victims, and found the Institute, where we had our French and English church services for five months past, wiped out, with the house adjoining, and the whole street choked quite three hundred yards away, and mangled bodies being carried out of the *débris*. Meanwhile another terrific crash, and I followed again in case help were needed—a house stood without a front, every room exposed to the street. I could not reach the third because the road was again blocked. The fourth I found a little way out of the village, and with some R.A.M.C. men and an officer who had boarded the car, found that a piece only of shell had completely wrecked a cottage. We searched among the wreckage, but found no one. In the field in front was an enormous hole, and at the bottom the base of a great seventeen inch shell. The officer got two of his men (they could hardly lift it between them) to put it on my car, and made me take it to the H.Q. for inspection. People were looking up at the sky for a Zeppelin ; but this was evidently a shell ; so as my *rôle* was rather specially the picking up of bomb victims (I used always to turn out on the first alarm, and cruise around in readiness) and as I was getting awfully tired, and the shells too numerous to chase, I went home and discussed

the situation with L.J., while the crashes continued to
shake the earth.

The clearing station was already on the move. We went
to the French hospital and found all in a panic. Two or
three sergeants were huddled, quivering, in a corner.
Several terrified orderlies were under the beds ; nurses and
doctors were sitting in a scared group in the middle of the
floor. Patients were screaming ; one had gone mad and
got out of bed stark naked. We went back and sent ten
cars to evacuate all the *blessés* that could be removed,
and returned later on. The big shells recommenced,
more terrifying in the dark, very close, and spattering
the building with *débris*. I was uneasy about my Napier,
and went to move it a little out of the town. Passed a
sentry, who whispered : "You fool ; that's just where
they're falling ! " Leaving the 'bus a little further on, I
went back to stay by my friends. We thought it was
the end. About 1 a.m. the *Infirmière-major* let me take her
and her staff to their billet and at 1.30 a.m. I turned into
our place in the centre of the town.

I expected to find the large hall full of people, and had a
little supper as quiet as a mouse, and lay down for the
night. L.J. came in looking for me, and told me every
one had evacuated to the *château*. I was too tired to move.
At 5 a.m. I was up and away on the Napier to our outpost
again. The streams of wounded have thinned ; and we
have had more help, but to-day the shelling has been
heavier, and we have had another evening of it at the base.
I was out at the *château* and watched the great clouds of
smoke and *débris* thrown up, in comparative safety. To-day
is the first day quiet enough to give one a moment's rest.
Can you wonder at my thankfulness for a little peace and
quiet this evening ? ˙

F.A.U.,

June 4th, 1915.

We find out here that cheerfulness under all conditions
is the most essential part of a soldier's equipment, or at any
rate the ambulance man's. During an attack when the

wounded are pouring in, and one hasn't slept, washed, shaved, or properly eaten for, say, thirty-six hours, you would think, to see and hear us, that we were having *the* time of our lives. . . . We worked at frightful pressure for about a month, but things are much quieter now, although one is still kept quite busy. The French lines particularly are very still. We are using the occasion to refit the cars. Our French work has continued uninterrupted just as before, except of course that it necessarily varies enormously in volume according to the fighting. Army movements now necessitate withdrawal of the B.R.C.S. Corps to ———. The men wanted me to stick to them, but that would have meant entire separation from the F.A.U. The advent of F.A.U. cars has meant my occupying myself a good deal with the civilian work which has now become the chief activity of the Unit, and with which I had nothing whatever to do before. We have by no means lost touch with the Army, however. I daresay I am not the only one who will long remember Whitsuntide, 1915. It was not a big affair, but very sharp while it lasted—what in military jargon is called a " smart tap " by the Germans. I was sleeping as usual out under the stars, when I was awakened *bene mane*, and told our dressing station at Ypres was calling for all available cars. I sprang up and started winding my Crossley—she was frightfully stiff to swing that morning, and by and by I sat down and quietly fainted. On coming to I was away to Y———. 'Twas Whit-Monday, and for the next twelve hours we worked through terrific heat, and noise and dust, evacuating from the aid-posts on the Lille and Menin roads. The bombardment was very heavy throughout the day, heaps of mutilated bodies at the ambulances, and in the Grand Place itself men and horses. The main road was one unending stream of wounded. Gas everywhere making throat and eyes smart, and on the turf outside our little dressing station at the *Augustinstraat* lay many a poor gassed Tommy from the trenches, whose smart was over for ever.

" STANDARDIZED " DAYS AT H.Q.

August 29th, 1915.

The summer has been quiet from a military point of view, as of course you know from the newspapers. We have been very busy, with work continually extending, and personnel increasing, so that the general quietness has not had any great effect upon us.

At P—— we have opened a clearing station for civilians, and at several villages just behind the lines, where the civilians are under shell-fire, we have small stations with a doctor, dresser, orderly, ambulance and driver. Here there is a regular *clientèle* of sick, who are visited in their homes ; and the wounded are immediately attended to, transported to our civilian clearing hospital, and passed on as soon as possible to the civilian base hospital. Each of these little out-stations has to have its dug-out in case of shelling. Last week we received several shells in the garden of the Belgian military hospital at P——, but up to the present we are continuing work in the cellars.

The latest activity is the search party, which constantly makes rounds of the villages along the front, tracing and notifying infectious diseases, dealing with infected water supplies, etc., etc. In all we have about seventy-five motors now, the very latest addition being a new " Ford " belonging to the Adjutant,* which became essential to him in the execution of his duties ! The standardizing, if I may use the expression, of our various activities, has led to life becoming much more normal for us all out here, except just at the times of rush that we have had now and again.

It amuses me to reflect that I came out here without a hair brush, thinking it would be an entirely superfluous luxury ! It was not until late in March that I went so far

* C.C. had been promoted to the post of Adjutant of the Unit.

as to procure a pair of pyjamas ! But as one settles, and as the Unit settles, into more or less regular work, it is senseless to keep up a pretence of roughing it.   Since May (Whit-Monday was the last engagement of any importance that we have had active part in) life has been almost normal at the base, and all except the smaller out-stations very near the trenches.   The whole thing is much like a large business concern.   It is a little difficult to the average member to get an idea of the work as a whole.   He gets into his little groove, works in it like a fine nigger, but in the nature of things has little opportunity for a wider outlook.

I accepted recently the post of Adjutant with a deep sense of responsibility, and now that I have a car of my own I am able to keep a necessary oversight upon our activities as a whole.   I have a certain amount of interviewing of authorities to do, and the inspecting work mentioned above. My chief asset from the promotion is the large voice I have in affairs.

It is all very interesting in a way ; but there is always an aching longing for the end of it all.   One feels that the best of the manhood of Europe is just being prostituted— all its fine energies being diverted from their true courses— and although one's work is a little endeavour to patch up some of the rents, one's own true work is just held up, inevitably, till the nightmare come to an end.   The winter is certain to bring an access of work, even if the autumn does not disturb the present equanimity, and so we are all busy preparing, and trying to dedicate ourselves afresh to the work.   It is so hard to keep the purity of purpose.

.   .   .

We have lost some men to the army, but generally speaking the spirit is right, and a strong feeling of *esprit de corps* and loyalty to the Society exists.   Here at H.Q. life is much less vivid than at the front, and nothing less than a sense of duty in accepting this promotion would have weighed with me.   There is not the same dear intimacy with *blessés*, *brancardiers*, doctors, nurses, which makes a happy family of the staffs in the danger zones, where common work, effort, risks, draw men together, create a sense of brotherhood, even in the army ! Here at a great barracks-hotel, swarming and ever changing as men come and go, are drafted here and there, it is very different. But with a sigh, one tries to think that one is glad to be where most wanted—and there is an end of it. Here, too, we have our occasional thrills of various kinds, but they are not frequent. Little red flags bristle all over the town, marking vaulted cellars, with doors opening up to the street, and there is a wonderful siren nicknamed " the cow ", which bellows at a touch from a button in the trenches twenty miles away when a great weapon—I dare not say any more.

October 17th, 1915.

How differently things have turned out from what we anticipated when we left England a year ago ! Then we thought the war would be over in a few months, at most. Our inspiration then, was the prospect of sharing, in the cause of Peace, all the dangers and hardships of the fighting soldier. This has been found quite impossible (except to some small extent for the small proportion of men who, like myself last winter and spring, had the privilege of being at the front). We thought we should be going out into the battlefield during, or immediately after a fight, dressing the wounds, carrying men home ; going, perhaps, between the very trenches for the wounded lying there. We thought we should come back home in about the same proportion as the regular army.

If it has been a disappointment that these anticipations have not been realized, it is because we have not realized that it is, to true men, a greater thing to *live* for a good cause than to *die* for it, and requires a higher order of courage.

I feel more and more that we who have been spared are only justified in going on living if our future lives manifest, at every point and at all times, a heroism *at least* equal to that of the soldier who is killed in battle.

I find my inspiration is chiefly in going cheerfully and patiently on, day after day, and week after week, with work that has become deadly monotonous ; being always bright, in spite of the appalling tragedy, and all that tends to depress.

One hates to have such a comparatively comfortable time as we (at H.Q.) are having now, sleeping in beds, enjoying food as good as we mostly get at home, whilst friends are in the trenches. Still, sacrifice seems of little use for its own sake—probably we could not have gone on living as we lived a year ago, and kept in health. I am still excessively busy, and on the whole very glad that it is so. I have no time whatever to read and very little to write.

November 7th, 1915.

I am more and more surprised and troubled at the slow progress of the war. Last winter I firmly believed it could not last beyond the summer, and now here we are forming the same pious hopes for another.

I am getting very soul-sick of the work out here the last four months of mending motor-cars instead of men.

It is tremendously brave of G—— to hold on with his work when the position of those young men who are still at home must have become extremely difficult. I wonder, and should like to hear, whether he has been caused any trouble by pressure to enlist ?

This winter, odd moments are being filled up with concerts, debates, football, badminton, drill,—it is all so astonishingly different from last winter, when one lay down on the straw in boots, after twelve, twenty-four, thirty-six or sometimes even more hours' work, and ate in cars on a journey or any other odd moment.

I wonder how long it would take the world to settle down to war as the normal state of things ? Not long, I fancy—another year would suffice, and it would be like adjusting one's self to slide as comfortably as possible down a slope into hell. Let us all pray with all the fervour of our beings that the end come before that deadly inevitable

6

motion begins. Let us struggle on yet, and make the world struggle, on the brink, against the tendency to slide over.

December 3rd, 1915.

In your last letter you plunge right into a matter which I feel rather keenly—by asking whether I am as happy now as last winter, when things were so much more thrilling, uncomfortable, disorganized. No, never again I fear will such times come for me. The whole war is organized like a huge business now, and even if movements occurred to upset the regularity and system of our present existence, I should be hopelessly fixed administratively in the H.Q. offices, and not executively labouring close in the wake of the combatants.

I see no hope whatever of ever being able to write a picturesque or interesting letter again. What can one say about eternal interviews with officials, settlings of disputes, payment of bills? Talk of sacrifice! I made mine when I put these stripes on my arm, and took a seat in the central office—not when I drove my ambulance under shell and rifle fire up to the trenches.

However, duty before all, and one never knows what may turn up one day, with all the regularity. I like to cheer myself up with the thought that the whole ghastly business *might* end as suddenly one day as it began. That is the day I long for above all. It is now nearly 11 p.m. I have had another Sunday entirely of work, all running about, seeing people, composing letters, etc. Yesterday afternoon I went over a lovely large French hospital some distance away which I had never visited before. These little diversions make life more interesting, and it is a great pleasure to me to be able once again to pay a visit to the wounded from time to time with cigarettes and chocolates. I have also undertaken to provide forty coverlets for Mme ——— (matron of a French hospital near by) like those at our Queen Alexandra hospital— very pretty printed cotton ones, which make a " *salle* " look so much more gay.

December 7th.

I feel that my work here will have to change soon, or else I shall have to go elsewhere. I should be more content as a hospital orderly than doing the work I have had to do during the last six months ; a hospital orderly is the lowest grade in our social scale, but you know why I should be content therewith. Often I have gone about my work all day with a pathetic longing to find someone to be kind to, gentle and loving with. I have felt the funds of sympathy in me drying up, for want of exercise. Two thoughts have been much in my mind lately. One is the possibility of returning to my ordinary civilian work, and taking my stand with those who are resisting pressure for military service. Of course I came out over thirteen months ago, before there was any ignominy resting upon those who stayed, and when we thought that the war would be ended in a few months. Having made my choice then, from a sense of conviction, I do not think there is any reason to change it and return, unless I feel clear that I can be serving a more useful purpose than I am doing out here. The other is Serbia. Ever since the new attack began upon that poor little country I have felt an immense " *attirance* " to go there—first with the military, realizing from experience out here a year ago, when everything was disorganized, what terrific need there must be for any ambulance work that could be rendered ; then later, and especially since I heard of the " War Victims " workers who had gone out there, my thoughts have envisaged the possibility of civilian relief work as an alternative ; God knows what the need for that must be just now ! I hope to be at home in January, but as the time is short it is as well to make enquiry beforehand.

THE ADJOURNED YEARLY MEETING

EDITOR'S NOTE.—In January 1916, an adjourned Yearly Meeting of the Society of Friends was held to consider the position of the Society in view of the passing of the Compulsory Military Service Act. C.C. happened to be at home on leave from the front at the time, and afterwards gave the following account of the gathering to his colleagues in France.

IN trying to give you some small idea of the Yearly Meeting at which I have had the privilege of being present, I cannot do better than ask you to read, slowly and thoughtfully, the " Statement " adopted by that gathering. . . .

Take it sentence by sentence, and each smallest phrase will be found to hold a truth which men would lay down their lives rather than deny. " We . . . re-affirm our entire opposition to compulsory military service." " War involves a surrender of the Christian ideal." " War involves the denial of human brotherhood." "Freedom from the scourge of war will only be brought about by the faithfulness of individuals to their utmost convictions." " We regard the act as imperilling the liberty of the individual conscience." " This liberty is the main hope of human progress." " A human tribunal is not an adequate judge of any man's conscience." And so on, all through.

It was a supreme opportunity. From the first a high spiritual note was struck. We considered the claims of the State upon us. Friends in the past have not been regardless of them. " But," as someone said, " is what the State requires one to do something which will help or hinder the coming of the Kingdom of God on earth ? Friends, *there can be no conflict of loyalties !* "

Out here in France each one must have realized the dangers of losing our hold on spiritual things, of starving for want of these and the intellectual advantages that mean so much to us at home. We are submerged in a system where material is supreme ; we are in a maelstrom where material struggles with material, and in the swirl and confusion *our* struggle is to keep hold of those divine cords of the spiritual life that alone can keep us afloat and draw us through the rapids we have voluntarily entered on to the solid rock.

Many of us came out here in the early days of the war—the horror of it throbbing in our brain, driving us to madness, or to the anæsthetic of intense activity. At home we saw no hope of the second alternative. On the battlefield, amidst suffering and death, something convinced us in spite of the haunting arguments brought by ourselves and others against it, there *must* be a place for the true follower of the Prince of Peace, with a heart full of love for those fellow men who have answered a call of duty different from his own.

We did right to respond. It was the answer, the impulse of the human heart ; an assertion that the supreme testimony of peace is a life lived in that spirit which takes away the occasion of all war. It is not our fault that opportunities for the service we desired have not always been opened for us, that the work has often been humdrum and monotonous—we answered the call and then waited, doing what was immediately required until the supreme opportunity should come. Let each man's conscience answer for the spirit of his waiting, for the unsullied purity of his first impulses through the difficult days.

I want you to imagine the shock to one coming from this hell of the material at the front into the heaven of the spiritual at Bishopsgate : where policemen answer the questions of the curious about the streams of quiet, earnest people issuing from the " tunnel ". " It's the Quakers," —and where one constable was heard to remark, " I dunno but what it would save a world o' trouble if everybody was like them folk ! "

In that wonderful atmosphere of love, and amid the

stirring of divine purposes, one felt and lived as one had never done before. What then had happened ? When *we* found a way prepared for peace work at the front, we accepted it with a deep sense of privilege. We felt that from our friends at home so great an opportunity for self-sacrificing service was immediately withheld. The reality is this : these weeks and months while we have been out here, *they* have been quietly, steadily working, organizing, above all *thinking* for peace at home. And now *their* time has come. And their testimony is going to be *the* peace testimony of the Society. Ours is and has been good pure testimony for peace. But it is a side show. When we came out we did not perhaps quite realize this. We thought sympathetically of the men who stayed at home, refusing the pressure to enlist, going quietly on with their work, and we longed for a sense of unity with them. But we only now grasp the terrific positive power that they have been generating and storing. We saw no way of making a stand for peace at home, which would absorb the passion with which we burned. It was indeed difficult. *They* bided their time, and it has come. The Government have given them their opportunity, and if our statesmen really mean to saddle the land with militarism, this will be the worst day's work they have done for many a long day.

And now those Friends who have risen to meet this great occasion turn with a welcome of comradeship to us out here.

" We do not feel that Friends who accept alternative service will compromise our case," said the spokesman of a great gathering of 451 young men. . . . Later another speaker of enlistment age said, " It is not a question of the methods of England or of Germany, but of the methods of God as against the methods of the world. Any service to which we put our hand must have as its direct object the establishment of the Kingdom of Jesus Christ, and such would not be less truly national service. This is not a *national* service Act, but a *military* service Act, and its direct

aim and object are the efficient prosecution of the war.
I cannot undertake alternative service under military
control, or any service which would aid the war.   May
there not be a real service to which we are called at this
time ? Has there not come to us some conception of the
passion of Jesus, when He saw people as sheep having no
shepherd, and do we not hear the call ' Feed my sheep ? '
If it were necessary in the time of the monks to say ' To
labour is to pray', it is now necessary to say that 'to pray
is to labour.' " . . . The sense of earnestness grew
and grew from moment to moment, rising to a wonderful
sustained yet quiet enthusiasm at the end.   One realized
that there was something much more than mere opposition
to an Act of Parliament.   Here were forces that had been
gathering, growing, shaping, in thinkers' minds for years.
On the ruins of the old rises ever the new.   The war, the
final downfall of all which men had lived and striven for,
may yet prove the birth of a new, sweeter, grander order
than the old which is passing away.

BACK AT DUNKERQUE—
THE CHALLENGE OF CONSCRIPTION

H.Q., F.A.U.,
12th March, 1916.

I am going to try to be a reformed character and write to you every week. All these weeks that I have been about in London, I have had a sort of feeling that my place was at the front. Now I am here again I hope I may settle down happily. It may be illogical, my being here. I did not come out at the end of a train of reasoning exactly. I could not see George Fox clearly in the war zone—but somehow or other I never failed to see Jesus Christ here, and it was an impulse to follow the Prince of Peace. " Ah, you have gone out to save life, not to kill," said Sir W. P. Byles to me the other day—and the good old white-haired man, saddened because so much that he has lived for has gone in these tragic days, put into words the thought that has so often been my motive force.

We had a still crossing, and the heavy snow of London turned to rain half-way over. Then at a port " Somewhere in France " snow was falling again, and the cheery greeting of the good folk at the Hotel des Voyageurs counterbalanced an otherwise very desolate " *salve* " to the continent. The little waitress came in dimpling as usual with the dinner, as though the world had no trouble, and France had never heard of Verdun. " *Pourquoi rigolez-vous?* " I asked in my best French slang. " *J'ne sais pas,*" " *Je rigole toujours,*" it is quite true, thought I, and very charming. Then I added aloud, " *Ça fait du bien,*" and she went off giggling into the kitchen to tell the other maids what monsieur had said !

By 8 p.m. we were starting on our night drive in my little Ford to H.Q. Snow was heavily on the ground and in the air throughout, and the great sweeping hillsides were very black and inhospitable. We had engine troubles, but struggled along, arriving about 11 p.m., tired and cold. The Hotel du Kursaal was very full, boys sleeping on the floor in several rooms, so I went on to the Alexandra Hospital.

It seemed in some ways almost like coming home again, old ———— has grown so familiar during these seventeen months of our acquaintance (the censor leaves you in some little doubt as to whether I refer to a place or a person !) I was thinking of the town—but of course people more than places make a home. Be sure that at the first opportunity I went round to see some of my friends, shopkeepers with whom I was acquainted as long ago as autumn, 1914. How generous in their friendship are these kind folk—so genuinely pleased to see one again, so simple. Everybody in England had been talking of the great offensive, the supreme defence. In France, nobody. Or, if so, with hushed breath, and " Ce n'est pas encore fini ". Ah, is it to be wondered at, when each day, whatever its other results, means thousands of desolate homes ? " Tous mes parents sont la-bas," said a man sadly ; already news that several had fallen.

In the streets, the women and little slips of girls wearing that terrible " deuil " which seems to enshrine the pale, tragic set little faces in such a wondrous dignity—the dignity of suffering—seemed to have increased noticeably in number, even during my brief absence. These gay folk are oh so solemn now !

I found both the ambulance convoys " en repos " ; one here at H.Q., and the other at a village half-way between here and the front. Both are busy refitting thoroughly for the coming season (what a ghastly word to slip out—but spring is indeed the season for slaughter in the Zone des Armées).

To-day a boy has come into the Queen Alexandra

Hospital, whose job, above all others, I think I should choose to do if I had only myself to think of. There is a dear old white-haired Colonel—soldier-Christian type, with the most generous heart in the world. Somehow or other, no one quite knows how, he has got into the shell-zone with a field-kitchen, and pitched out in a little wood alongside an ambulance, through which the wounded trickle (speaking of calm moments on the " *Front belge* ") on the journey from trench, four kilometres away, to the rail-head, fifteen kilometres or so in the rear. He asked for an assistant, and my boy has used himself up by working every day and most of every night (as any boy would wear out in. course of time—myself in longer time than most) helping in operations, dressings, orderly work at the ambulance, preparing and distributing Oxo, cocoa, chocolate and biscuits to the " *chers blessés* ", loading them into the motors, and, what costs so much more than everything else, cheering, loving, inspiring, *spending* himself for their other than material welfare, over and above all he has been able to do for *that*.

Some day that trickle will, alas, swell suddenly into a flood, and then away will go my little Ford, and I shall shake off the dust of offices and spread my ground sheet and blankets under the trees and stars for a few hours' sleep out of every twenty-four. I do not want that flood, but if it come, the joy of the thought that perhaps it may be my privilege to be there ! . . . How well I remember during the first six months of being out here, giving my wounded Germans chocolate, cigarettes, etc., by stealth. One could do a certain minimum openly, but the rest required care. We carried a young schoolmaster—I remember his great round-rimmed spectacles—away to die in a clean little hospital out of the reeking straw where he lay, and nearly got into serious trouble. A fiery little officer wanted him to be shot for alleged maltreatment of wounded, and hung about him like a bird of prey. God knows whether the young fellow was guilty. Anyway, he died a few hours later. So God will judge him.

H.Q., F.A.U.,
March 26th, 1916.

I see by the date of my last letter that it is a fortnight since I wrote to you. Thus perish good resolutions. But I have been very busy indeed. Very rarely in bed before 11.30 and breakfast at 7 a.m. This week, with the lighter mornings coming, parades begin two days a week at 6 a.m. There is a great deal of controversy in the Unit as to whether such things are not " pure militariness " without any adequate ulterior end. As usual the poor Adjutant gets the benefit of everyone's opinions, and some are pretty pronounced ! If he is not the embodiment of tact at the end of it all it will not be for want of a liberal education.

As I set out, there seems so little that can possibly interest you. One needs to live at a high pitch of inspiration in order to see colours through the spectacles of a sixteen hour routine day. Put me in a French town at the outset of a fortnight's summer holiday, and I will paint a picture or two. But at the end of seventeen months' forced acquaintance things are bound to lose the first blush of charm. I am compelled by honesty to admit that the *gamins* and *gamines* who still point out with such indefatigable originality that one is " Onglish", and have added " one pennish ", to the original " cigarette ishaplish " (if you please) in their *repertoire* of foreign phrases, appear just a trifle less *naïf* than they did in October 1914. Still, a walk to the town is still an adventure, interesting, if not thrilling, and your Adjutant readily suppresses a rather artificial dignity when grubby little fists are stuck into his, and walks along contentedly enough. Poor little mites ! I suppose it is the first time they have walked hand in hand with " *trois galons* ", and it may well be the last. Apart from the *gamins*, the town is full of interest, however. Crowded with folk of all descriptions, the housewives hatless and unkempt, the *gens de famille* in costumes of questionable elegance, the pathetic widows, and everywhere, immense background to everything, the " *bleu* horizon " of the now almost universal new French military uniform. And everywhere friends ! Tradespeople, officials, with whom one comes into almost daily contact, and with whom one passes always at least the cheery time of day and weather ; others who call for a tender little enquiry after madame, the *fils au front*, *à l'hôpital*, or what not, according to one's intimacy with their joys and sorrows, hopes and fears. Sometimes it is an ōld *camarade* of the " *Campagne des Flandres* " of the winter 1914-15, whom the kaleidoscope of war has thrown up to us again from some far distant section of the front where they had gone, as we thought, to be lost to us for ever. And that is a great joy, you may be sure, and almost certainly necessitates two little seats at the *estaminet* and two little glasses *pour trinquer*. Do not imagine that the little table scenes take place at any hour— only between 6 and 8 p.m. are the *estaminets* open, and for the rest poor *poilu* misses sorely his seat upon the *trottoir*. Sunday, however, is an exception, a great day, *un jour féeré*, one long blissful dream of strutting and sipping and gossip.

This letter, like its predecessor, is evidently fated to suffer serious delays—the last paragraph is already two days old, and I have forgotten all that I was going to say. We have had a couple more air raids since last I wrote. This is all in the nature of " Copy " that I have for you. We have rumours and counter rumours, to be sure, thrilling enough to keep us eager and alert for the moment when the preparation (of character, mainly) of all these months of dull routine may be put to the test. I wonder if any of you can understand the psychology of this " passion for sacrifice ", " rage to suffer " for mankind ? I cannot, but it is there somewhere within me ! Our friends are dying cheerfully and well. We see them marching straight, steadfast to do it, and may not share the privilege. We tell ourselves it is harder to *live* for a great cause than to *die* for it. But is it ? (The more one works, the greater one's aspirations, the deeper the joy of life. It is *good*, this life one lives, is going to live, in consecration to a great purpose.) Life is good for these young strong men here too, going up to the trenches—look at their fine healthy faces—and it's hard giving up any good thing.

I remember on the first day of Camp at Jordans (September 7th, 1914) saying to A.N.B. that the only thing that would give me more real joy than training for ambulance work at that moment would be going to prison for resisting conscription. I confess that now, after seeing and talking to the boys at the front for so many months, young, strong, full of life—still, pale, smashed, and near to death, and knowing in how many cases their course too has been a matter of conscience—I find it hard to realize the intense joy of the prophet as I did then. Resist I must and yield to none in the firmness of my resolve. But to me it is painful to have to stand aside whilst they march up to die for their cause ; my only sacrifice is the thirst for sacrifice unsatisfied. I know this is all wrong—it's so shortsighted. But if only one could suffer a little for one's cause !

I have seen to-day a circular from the Friends' Service Committee,* in which the poor unit has finally been disowned. It is rather sad, but a result I have seen to be inevitable since the passing of the Act. I am happy to believe that the Committee as individuals have no lack of sympathy with us as individuals, while being compelled for the sake of the stand they are making, to dissociate themselves, corporately, from us, corporately. Many of us here are really far more in sympathy with them than with ourselves, so to speak !

I hear that there are large numbers of new applicants for membership of the Unit. I am frankly sorry. I hoped that after the passing of the Act Friends would not wish

* The Friends' Service Committee was set up in 1915 (in view of the probable adoption of conscription by this country) to strengthen Peace Testimony and service among Friends of military age and to advise Friends in regard to their position under the Military Service Acts. The Committee from the first deprecated any compromise with Conscription, and gave an " Absolutist " lead, while leaving it to the individual to decide on his own conscience his own course of action.—Ed.

to join the Unit in large numbers. In so far as members
are non-Friends, I am more happy, so long as funds can
stand the strain. But I was grieved and shocked when at
home to find the Emergency Committee having to with-
draw little weekly grants from necessitous alien mothers
with large families, whilst vast sums subscribed by members
of the Society were going to maintain work which, pure in
principle and intrinsically good as it is, would yet be done
by the armies in our absence. I am most anxious that
earnest thought be given to the work to be taken up by
these new drafts. If we can get relief work (? Poland),
work on the land, or welfare work in munition factories
it will be, I am convinced, infinitely better than just taking
on more military work. I am *very* glad we have undertaken
what we have, but simply to multiply it would be a mistake.
If there was a real dangerous bit of peace work which the
authorities wanted us to undertake, it would be another
matter, but most of it is so dreadfully " *embusqué* ", as the
French say. There is tremendously good stuff in the Unit,
believe me, with all its failings, and the work it will do if
circumstances should change the present routine conditions,
might, I think, form a bright, if quixotic, page in the
Society's history. But like most precious material it
requires awfully careful handling.

A good many of my boys are getting restless, being
afraid that C.O.s will be forced either into the N.C.C. or
into prison, and that if so they must resign the F.A.U. and
take their share of the hardships.

I think at present such action would he hasty, and based
on insufficient premises. . . . I felt that we claimed
absolute exemption in order to plumb our action with that
of our friends at home. We hardly dared expect to get it,
because we made it absolutely clear that nothing conditional would do for us, and we were going to take the
consequences. Well, we got our "absolute", and I should
have thought we, having nothing more to do but carry on,
would do it. But no. It is this thirst for sacrifice, you see.
If not in Flanders, then at Pentonville. Well, I understand.

RESPONSE TO THE CHALLENGE—
"IN HONOUR BOUND"

Sunday, 14th May, 1916.

You will be anxious to hear how things are going on here.
Rather sadly. . . It has been dawning on me gradually
that the continuance of our work does in fact depend upon
the sinking of our individuality and stifling of our freedom
of expression. The Conscription Act has meant a gradual
tightening of the screw of military discipline, and I cannot
help feeling now that we are in effect a conscript unit—
with a more sympathetic control immediately above, to
be sure, but the iron hand lurking in the background.

I am sure for the great majority of men out here the Unit
is a good thing. They are young, and it is a right *via media*,
even since the Act. But I am equally convinced that the
time has come for some to leave. My great hope was that
the few who felt called to another service might go with the
blessing and sympathy of the entire Unit. This has not
been entirely realized. Some seem to be annoyed that
any could think of taking such action and tried to force
them into the position of rebels. I think we are living this
down and coming quietly and strongly into the sympathy
we hope for. My own position was peculiar. Whilst
sympathizing intensely with those who felt it right to leave,
I thought perhaps my duty might be to remain, owing to
my special position, and in spite of my sympathy with the
others. The "rebel" suggestion, and a growing realization of the changed circumstances into which the Act has
drawn us, moved me to take up a more emphatic attitude,
one which appeared hardly consistent with my remaining
one of the principal officers. I acted throughout from a
sense of deep concern,—loyalty to Pacifism and the Society
of Friends seeming a greater thing than to the Unit or the
Committee, I sent in my resignation of the adjutancy. I

am clear that the time has come for me to resign. I could have stayed on in spite of the conviction that the Unit is no longer a place for the strong peace man—but the later happenings make it impossible—as an ordinary member all excuse for my doing so finally disappears.

EDITOR'S NOTE.—After C.C. had severed his connection with the F.A.U. his certificate of " absolute " exemption, which had been granted by the War Office, was withdrawn. In due course he appeared before Local and Appeal Tribunals, voicing his conviction in the following words :

" Conscience does not primarily object and refuse, but commands. It commands loyalty to the voice of God in in the heart. I think this is the same thing, whether it be called religion or morality.

" I am not chiefly concerned to secure exemption from military service, but to bear witness to the Truth as it is revealed to me : knowing that I do this whether I obtain exemption or not, whether I am free in the body or not, so long as I remain true to principle.

" I have little desire for my own safety and comfort, when hundreds of thousands of my fellowmen of all nations are laying down their lives. Most strong young men to whom the ideal makes an appeal are possessed by a passion for adventure and sacrifice in a noble cause. I am no exception : I understand and honour those, my comrades, who have enlisted in the army to fight, as they believe for the right. The greatest sacrifice I have ever made is to withhold from sharing with them their sublime self-surrender. But I too am enlisted, not merely for three years or the duration of the war, under a Captain who also calls for adventure and sacrifice in His name : whose commands to me are unmistakable, not only to act towards enemies in a very different spirit, and to overcome them redemptively with very different weapons from those which are being used on the battlefields to-day ; but also to proclaim His commands and to win recruits to His cause.

" It is deeply painful for one who has tried, however falteringly, to give his whole life in joyful service for God and humanity, to find his allegiance to the law of the State in jeopardy. For the first time in my life I have become acutely conscious that the command of the State may be for me no longer compatible with the command of God, to whom loyalty is supreme. Maybe, because although I cannot undertake ' alternative service ' under the Conscription Act (for this would imply a bargain with militarism, which I believe to be utterly wrong), nevertheless I would respectfully remind the Tribunal that, provided they are satisfied with the genuineness of my conscientious conviction, the Act (Section 2, 4.3) and Government instructions for its administration, enable them to grant me absolute exemption."

Whilst acknowledging the reality of his conscientious objection, both Tribunals refused the " absolute " certificate for which from the first he had consistently asked. Since his return from France C.C. had taken up work at Woodbrooke Settlement, Birmingham, becoming chairman of a group for the study of International Relations and general work of Reconstruction ; he continued quietly at his work awaiting the arrest which now seemed inevitable.

THE HOME FRONT—
" MARCHING UP "

The Police Cells,
Birmingham.

THINGS have happened rather breathlessly in the last day or two, and I must now, at leisure, smooth out the story a little for you dear ones, saying by way of preface, that I think I have never in all my life experienced a purer happiness than I do as I write. On Tuesday last the detective called for one of our men—. . . a dear fellow —and one or two others went down to the Police Court with him on the following day. One of these was an absentee and was nipped in the bud ; the other was closely questioned about Woodbrooke and who was there. On Friday, whilst we were at lunch half a dozen soldiers and officers and two detectives suddenly appeared at the dining room door, and asked for the Warden. I could not escape the impression, " They are come with swords and staves ". After lunch we had the round up, and all who were liable had to go down immediately to the Recruiting Office. After an hour or so we were taken to the Police Cells and locked up, the Army Captain who had dealt with us refusing us leave until the next morning, when we were due to appear before the Beak. However, Mr. W——— came down and succeeded in obtaining remand on bail in £5 each from the civil authorities. This was a great mercy as I had immense stacks of things to settle up before my departure. The eight of us then had a jolly tea with Mr. W———, and about 6 p.m. I parted from the others—they going straight back to Woodbrooke, I making a few purchases in the way of parting presents to special friends ; I got back to Woodbrooke just in time for dinner, and then I wired into business like wildfire. . . . After the evening hymn we—all the men students—had cocoa and biscuits in B———'s drawing room, and a time of worship afterwards. Then I went on straightening up affairs, and finished towards breakfast-time. Immediately after devotional, we went down again to the police courts and were " fined " and handed over to the military ; we were taken to the recruiting station again, an immense hall (an old theatre) surrounded by tiers of little offices, from which we move on and on, round and round in a tedious succession. I did not trouble to find out exactly what was happening. It was rather interesting to watch pensively the big machine at work, and restful to be tranquil and have to do nothing on one's own initiative. Endless papers had to be filled in at each office, at the end of which the clerk (they are mostly W.V.R. women, some of whom attempted weak humour at our expense) said, " You refuse to sign ? " so even that step, or absence of it, was taken for one. About 4.30 we were through and taken before the Captain, who said our escorts to Worcester would not arrive before Monday. This we had anticipated, and we had been given to expect that we should almost certainly be let out over the week-end. This, however, the Captain refused, and we were committed to the lock-up, where I am presently writing. . . . You know how I should have loved to see you again to say good-bye. However, in about ten weeks' time we shall be having our little chat through the bars at the Scrubs ! I forgot to say that large numbers of our friends were at the Police Court, and waited all day at the Recruiting Office for us. . . I was naturally rather tired after Friday night, and the standing about almost all day ; yesterday was very tiring too, but my feelings were of quiet peace, and a rather amused interest in all that was proceeding. Since coming here I have been filled with a quite absurd sense of joy and happiness. They do not lock us up except at night, and there is quite a good promenade space between the two rows of cells. I am sitting in this now, on the stone floor, back to the wall. There are a score or so of soldiers in the lock-up and half a dozen civilians, I mean on one tier—there are several tiers of cells. Nearly all the soldiers are absentees, and express their intention of remaining in " ' Klink ' for duration ". They are up to all sorts of tricks for attaining this end, and generously pass on all the best tips ! One is not surprised that they have a sense of fellowship with us, based though it is on such a profound misunderstanding. There is one poor soldier whose face is a picture of abject fear—it haunts me—he expects the death sentence at his court martial. . . We are two in a cell for the night. I slept quite a bit on the stone floor (and two rather lousy blankets) and feel quite fresh this morning. My friend called out at one point, " Are you asleep, Corder ? " " No, but I'm having a good time," was the reply. I was. . . .

When the gaoler unlocked the cell door in the morning and awoke me out of a nap, I cried, " Hello, Dad " (he's a nice old boy), and I had a strange feeling of being very much at home. We had a lovely little meeting in one of the cells last night before being locked in—at the same time that Woodbrooke was having its prayer meeting. The thought uppermost in our minds was, " Peace I leave with you, My Peace I give unto you, not as the world giveth give I unto you ; let not your heart be troubled neither let it be afraid." And we remembered that the promise was for *all* ; not for us, or for our friends only ; and especially for all who suffer and sorrow. We sang, " Jesus, the very thought of Thee ", and " How sweet the name of Jesus sounds ". A soldier and two civilians came in, and stayed quietly. The latter were gipsies who had been taken off their caravan for military service, and had been through the processes of the afternoon with us ; we had a sort of fellow feeling for them. Such nice bronzed faces, and clean, gentle speech. One told me he was stifled by the prison atmosphere after the " open road ", and I felt for him. The other had a sprained wrist from a fall on the icy road and was in considerable pain. I am writing to their wives to-day, neither of them can read or write. We had a big chunk of bread and cheese each at 8.30 p.m., and an immense mug of tea (2-pint) which was about one-third full, for which we paid 2d. each, as it was a luxury. I do not think I desire any better fare, though one might lack variety on such a diet in perpetuity! One of my continual complaints in the Unit was that the food was too good! We Unit men are going to score; boards to sleep on, minimum of convenience in sanitary matters, roughing it generally—these things were normal two years ago! We had a little meeting again this morning very helpfully, and I have been writing since. It is refreshing to be able to do things in a leisurely way! I think during the next fortnight I *may* catch up with my private correspondence for the first time in many years. . . . Books have been brought us, and this afternoon I may even get the privilege of a shave—my safety razor is put away in a docketed parcel with scissors, pocket knives and other dangerous implements. Every now and then a stentorian voice calls out, "One down", and there descends a newcomer. Stragglers came in during the night—drunks who made noise, some kicking their doors. To-morrow I think we shall go on to Worcester. Farewell, dear ones. My feeling is of the overwhelming love and kindness of God, and my friends.

EDITOR'S NOTE.—The Birmingham *Evening Despatch* for Saturday, January 13th, 1917, in the course of an account of the arrest and appearance in court of C.C. and his seven companions, contained the following paragraph: " A similar fine was inflicted upon the defendant Catchpool, who was said to be an absentee since January 8th. He preferred not to plead, and added : ' I count no man on earth my enemy, because God is the Father of all men, and we are all brothers. The life and teaching of Jesus Christ give me an unshakable faith in the redeeming power of love."

Guard-Room, ——— Barracks,
Worcester.

January 16th, 1917.

We were brought over here yesterday from Birmingham, but before I describe present surroundings, let me take up the story where I left off in my last letter. We did not have a very good night again, the two blankets dealt out to each of us were very dirty—it was a choice between fleas and freeze. The former won easily, as you will discover if the alternative is ever put to you ! In the morning we had breakfast in the cells, and our little time of worship together was very helpful. Writing was almost impossible, as there was almost constant marshalling of prisoners for the police court which begins at 11 o'clock. We, of course, had been dealt with on Saturday, but were moved about with the others and so had little quiet. The previous evening a little army sergeant had got a razor and shaving soap smuggled in, and did a roaring trade at the barber's business (subsequently losing all his profits at cards, which the soldiers play incessantly). . . . About 11.15 our escort arrived, sixteen or so soldiers who were under the command of a sergeant. Several friends had heard the hour of our departure and were at Snow Hill to see us off. I hoped to get a glimpse of the Malvern Hills, which would have been an inspiration, but all was shrouded in mist. Arriving about 2.30 p.m., or rather earlier, we were put immediately into the guard room. First, however, we were made to give up everything we had with us, even all our pocket things—spectacles, scissors, knives, pencils, all our books and papers and toilet things. This was rather a blow, as it meant no writing or reading, nor shaving. In the guard-room we were greeted by two other C.O.s, who with us and eight soldiers, made eighteen men in a little room, in which one could take only eight short paces in one direction and five in the other !

There was not enough light to write or read by, and the only ventilation was through a little grating over the door. There was seating accommodation for about half the company at a time. It was just a matter of patience, waiting for something to happen. I wondered if this was " killing time ", remembering that one cannot do that without injuring eternity. However, I decided there was purpose in our waiting. About 5 p.m. tea made a diversion, a bucket and two " tots " (mugs), and a thick slice of bread and butter each. About 7 p.m. the eight new arrivals (i.e., we) were moved down into a sort of cellar, an old armoury—stone block floor, and musket racks all round the walls—very musty smell, and everything thick in dust. Three blankets apiece were brought in, the tiny gas jet made it quite obscure, and without books or anything to write with, and no chance of seeing if we had, there was nothing to do but to turn in ; it was bitterly cold, so none of us slept much : the army blankets were clean, but the Birmingham fleas " carried on ! " However, the longest night comes to an end. Breakfast was the same as tea. We had to walk about to keep warm. There was no sitting accommodation. We had a job to get permission to wash—one had thought the army had a greater concern for cleanliness. At last we were taken four at a time to a basin, but had neither soap nor towels. We had to knock and be escorted for the slightest motives for exit. About eleven this morning we were taken to the " Allocation Room ", and waited there an hour or so. They seemed in doubt what to do with us. Some of us had certificates of exemption, some none. As far as I could discover I was drafted to an infantry regiment—there seemed to be some doubt about my certificate. Of course it all comes to the same thing in the end, but we shall be split up, I fear— some may leave here to-day for various parts of the country, but we know nothing definitely. The old machine works along, and C.O.s drift through its mill without any serious friction. The soldiers are all sympathetic, the N.C.O.s harsh, the officers frigid but courteous. All is interesting, and the discomfort does not detract. I am so happy and cheerful. The week-end at the Police cells was a wonderful experience, and will be a precious memory. The sense of

God's presence, quickened by all we were undergoing, and
the almost overwhelming loving-kindness of all our friends,
made the little cells there very sanctuaries to us. The
difficulty lies in the lonely days ahead—if there *is* difficulty
(one almost begins to doubt it). How infinitely less, anyway, than the dear sufferers on the battlefields. You
know I would share to the utmost with them if duty called
me there. This that lies before me is the expression of my
sympathy with all who suffer and sorrow at this time.
The expression of my love for my dear country. It seems
little to give. But it is wrong to court sacrifice for its own
sake. I have been spared much—I must give much.
My friends at the front give their lives in one way—I must
give mine in another. I want these experiences to make
me fitter for a life dedicated to the service of God and men.
The path of you dear people who are striving to live such
a life at home may well be more difficult than my own—
my prayer is that it may not be less happy.

Guard-Room, ——— Barracks,
Worcester,
8 a.m., *January 18th, 1917.*

Just as we were settling down for the night yesterday,
an N.C.O. came and said, "To-morrow morning at
7.30 a.m., seven leave with draft. Pte. ——— stands fast."
Apparently there is some slight difference in the wording
of Pte. ———'s certificate, which puts him into the N.C.C.,
and the rest of us into the fighting forces.

This is a distribution centre, so the machine has to
distribute us. Whether we seven shall all go together, or
be further "distributed", we do not know, nor do we
know where we are going, although we may start any
minute now. Rumour says Southampton, and again
rumour says Woolwich, but rumour is often a lying jade.
Here we have had a time full of interest—my only trouble
is lack of sleep. I can't do it packed like herrings in a tub ;

the hard floor gives me little trouble, as I am used to that in the Unit. The whole life reminds me constantly of early Unit billets—it is not at all unlike, except no freedom here, and only one half-hour in the open air since arrival. An N.C.O. and three men live, move and have their being with us, and are changed every twenty-four hours. It might hurt one's feelings to be so suspect if we did not know that by the men themselves we are not the least bit suspect ; they are constantly apologizing for the old machine which alone actuates their movements. We have had wonderful experience with our guards, they come in frigid and a trifle suspicious, and leave after twenty-four hours, the best of friends. The C.O. attitude appears perfectly natural to them, in their own way many of them even understand it. Some don't even trouble to understand it, but take you at your face value of a good fellow, and give you the same in return. Foul-mouthed, as practically everyone in the army is, they have as kind heart at bottom as you could wish. (Most of them have been out to the front and wounded once or twice. I have great talks with those who know places where I have been. Not one has any delusions left about the war, such as one meets everywhere from civilians at home, every man of them wants the end, and doesn't care a toss how it is arrived at.) The corporal last night—bluff, unsentimental as a stone, blurted out a few words of very sincere regret when he heard we had to go. Each evening we have asked, " Have you any objection to our having a little meeting ? " " Do just whatever you like." And as we read a few verses, sung a hymn or two, and had a few words of prayer, the foul talk stopped, absolute quiet reigned, and the soldiers' heads were bowed. We were told that the men in the Guard Room were putting in applications to take charge of us ! They gave us a quiet " Good luck to you wherever you go ! " when we left.

This morning we were given lunch packets for our journey, all beautifully done up. The sergeant in charge of us (I am finishing this in the train) was wild because

an escort was told off to guard us on the journey. He
said he was quite sure that we should give less trouble than
the ordinary batches of recruits, who are simply in charge
of a sergeant. Since starting we have discovered we are
bound for Woolwich.

In the Train,
Waterloo to Portsmouth.
January 19th, 1917.

It seemed funny to me yesterday to be in London again,
piloting our poor be-muddled sergeant, his escort, our six,
and eleven other conscripts, through the complications
of tubes and other London transit difficulties. We got
down to Woolwich about 4.30 p.m., a damp, dismal
afternoon. After the rolling snow-clad hills through
which we had wended in the morning sunlight, the dull
streets seemed very unattractive, and the long waits in
the cold were trying. We got to the depot at last—acres
and acres of barracks, about which we were directed from
one place to another. At length we halted in a large
stone-paved yard, whilst the sergeant went inside. We
stood patiently in the cold again, and then to our joy were
all taken into a mess-room and enjoyed first-class bread and
jam, and hot tea. A corporal, upon hearing that we were
C.O.s took it upon himself to make extremely offensive
remarks in foul language and a loud voice for the benefit
of the whole room—ending by telling the company that
the O.C. had ordered us to be ironed and put in the cells
for the night—which (evidently feeling that he had not
quite made the most of his opportunities) he immediately
amended to " chained out on the common all night "—
which rather gave the show away. We felt rather sorry
for him, but concluded that his remarks were probably
being addressed less to us, than to the rest of the room,
which was full of conscripts. Immediately the blustering
corporal had disappeared, another came up quietly to our
table and began chatting in a most friendly way—evidently

—very obviously—meaning to be kind and soothe the feelings he thought must have been hurt. He started it on the weather, dear man, and ended in a stage whisper that we mustn't take any notice of what the other man said ! As soon as we had fed, the sergt.-major came and told our sergeant to follow with us. I overheard scraps of conversation—" Going on first thing in the morning," etc. We were taken to a large room with stove just lighted, coal supply and bedding, three blankets each, and three " biscuits "—the popular name for the mattress squares, three of which make up a full-sized mattress. So instead of a night on the common we had mattresses for the first time since arrest! The room was dimly lighted, but we sat round the stove and had our little time of worship by its light.

This morning we were called at 6.30, and taken down to the guard room, where we waited till about 8.30. The guards were having breakfast, and we were given to understand that ours was to be brought down. We had rather a tedious wait. At first in silence, then the soldiers began to talk ; one said, " Good job all the world isn't the same in morals and character "—one wondered what was coming next—" there'd be nothing but fighting and bloodshed if all was like me ! " This man was troubled at the delay in the arrival of our breakfast, and went on his own to see the sergeant about it. The others were more distinctly sympathetic. They all shook hands very warmly as we left—" So long, chummy ! " " Good-bye and good luck," were the typical farewells. Our old sergeant and escort of the night before re-appeared and conducted the same party to Waterloo. The poor man is a regular old woman, *we* are really taking charge of *him*, the escort and the eleven other conscripts ! I tell him how to get to where he wants to go. We carry his documents, take care of his tickets for him, etc. ; he is in mortal fear of losing them. He constantly says, " For heaven's sake, don't let me forget this, or that." The escort is still rankling in his mind, and he soon reverted to it again—in

fact, he seemed so depressed that we had to keep saying,
" Cheer up, sergeant ".   He puts the escort in a separate
compartment ; and then, as he confessed to us, is in terror
lest *they* should " hop it ! " Any of us could have made off
a hundred times yesterday or to-day with the most perfect
and sedate ease.   We are now in a most comfortable
second-class carriage, *en route* from Waterloo to Portsmouth
—we seven and our old sergeant, who is dozing over my
Daily News and puffing his old pipe.

> The First-class Waiting-room,
> Reading Station.
> 10 a.m.
> *January 20th, 1917.*

I continue the journal of my experience in the army
from the above unexpected *mise-en-scène.*   I think I left
you in the train going from Waterloo to Portsmouth.   The
journey ended as comfortably as it began ; we were a
pleasant little party, we seven and our old grandmotherly
sergeant, in a comfortable second-class lavatory carriage.
We alighted at ——— and walked about a mile to the
——— Barracks.   At the great doors—through which
one had a glimpse of an immense parade ground covered .
with guns and teams, horse and foot being trained to man
them, one felt again a brief moment of trepidation at the
thought of the reception of a " C.O." at such a place,
which we believed was to be our court-martial home, and
where no C.O. had ever set foot before.   In we went, and
were taken to a large upstairs room full of clerks, where
the gunners among us were put aside from the drivers.
Then our sergeant, who always did the gentleman in this
respect, took the sergeant-major (i.e., the N.C.O. in charge
of the depot) aside, and explained that seven of us were
C.O.s, that we had given no trouble whatever, were good
chaps, etc., etc.
Then we seven were set aside from the rest, and the

Captain sent for, to see us. He was a kindly man of the country squire type, followed about everywhere by a fine dog. He said he did not know what on earth to do with us. " We'll take them into the army, Sir, if they're willing to join," prompted his sergeant-major. I thought of saving time by advising him what was the proper thing to do with us, but he was already asking us formally and very rapidly—assuming the negative—whether we would join the army (which we were already " deemed " by law to have joined !) Then again he was nonplussed, and said we should only give him unnecessary trouble if we stayed there. I said, " We don't want to cause any unnecessary trouble." In a moment his mind was made up. " No trouble, my boy, I'm going to send you all back again where you came from. Just go down and wait on the parade ground, while I make arrangements for you. It's cold, walk about to keep warm if you like ; better not smoke." The sergeant-major, the class of man usually down on C.O.s, came along and eyed us. " You're a funny lot," he said, wagging his head at us (not after the manner of the Pharisees, but with a little twinkle of the eye and twitch of the mouth that betrayed a kind heart in spite of himself). " I've had six hundred recruits through my hands to-day : what should I have done if they'd all been like you ? " One felt a measure of sympathy with him in the predicament foreshadowed ! Then, the Captain came back and said cheerily, " Now, boys, you're going back to Worcester at six o'clock ; you've got a couple of hours, I'll give you some tea before you go ; run upstairs into the warm while it's got ready." By and by we were enjoying great basins of steaming tea and bread and jam *ad lib.* in a spotless mess room. Captain ——— came in again to look at us, and stood chatting. " Where do you chaps come from ? " etc., then, " What on earth did they want to bring you into the army for ? " We told him we were students from a College in Birmingham, and again said we had no wish to give trouble. " Better have left you there—all I'm sorry for is to see such a fine lot of chaps as you in trouble."

We told him our prospective pathway through the Scrubs, at which he commented, " I'd rather have a bullet in France than that." Finally, before he left us, he said, " Now, boys, you've got a long wait ; do you smoke ? make yourselves comfortable, good-bye!" After a pleasant time round the fire our brief visit to Portsmouth came to an end, and we marched back to the station feeling again that our path had been wonderfully and unexpectedly made smooth. It appears that the regiment was " closed ", full up the day we left Worcester, and the wire came just too late. When we arrived at Woolwich a wire was waiting for us telling us to proceed to Portsmouth. They, too, were full up, so the whole eighteen of us, seven C.O.s and eleven other conscripts, had to return to our original depot at Worcester. It was like going home again after our wanderings, and we were all very cheerful at the prospect.

We spent the night at Reading Barracks, sleeping on well-stuffed straw mattresses, like trying to roost on a cylinder. As we were getting up a newspaper boy came in selling papers, so we shared a *Daily News* whilst sitting round the fire waiting for brekker, and read the leading article. Ah, me ! newspapers in war-time ! as I read that article of blood and iron, I was not dissatisfied to be a prisoner for my faith, though for it, I have as yet, suffered hardly any discomfort. Women rail a little sometimes as we go through the streets, and if there be any ordeal in our position, it is outside the army, not inside.

" There's not one in a thousand has the courage to stand by his conscience," said a soldier to me yesterday. I have food for thought when I contrast this attitude of the men themselves with civilians I have met ; men and women who have thrown themselves into a passion of rage when I have handed them a picture of Christ on the Cross, with the words, " In Christ's Name, Peace,"—and have torn it up under my eyes.

The Scrubs is still ahead, an unknown quantity, and if the war lasts long (which God forbid for others' sake) the trial may be very severe. Still, as I return "home" to Worcester this morning, and think of that article in to-day's *D.N.*, I face the future should the trial even be death, with a glad calm and peace of mind, with a great confidence that there is a better way of adjusting whatever it may be that is wrong with the world.

IN THE "DUG-OUT"

Guard-Room,
Worcester.
January 21st, 1917.

I MUST tell you a little about our journey yesterday. The sergeant and I were the only ones of our party in the carriage, the other occupants being civilians. Two were Shrewsbury boys returning to school, full of cadet corps, of the fifty boys who had " joined up " during the vacation, and things military in general. They were having a great time discussing such things with our sergeant and the compartment at large. Suddenly they were relating with great relish the story of the " Conscientious Objector at Harrow ". " They all went at him with pens painted white —white feathers, you know." The older boy was sitting next to me, so I withdrew from my letter, looked at him and said quietly, " Seven of us are C.O.s—*I'm* one of them." He gave a little sort of gasp, and collapsed, but said nothing, and I'm afraid I had done for the military conversation, as it was not resumed before we separated. At Worcester it was drizzling, and we were not sorry to see the old barracks again. They had a home-like sort of feeling about them, though after the semi-freedom of two days' travel we soon began to realize that " home " was a prison after all. We were taken down to our cellar—the " Dug-out " we have christened it—and locked into the inner of the two rooms. It was bitterly cold and we just stood about (there was no room to locomote, we should have been like the bombarding molecules of a gas). We had to give up all our possessions again, turn pockets out, as well as deliver parcels—and the results of two days' patient smuggling (our previous two days here) have been wiped out. One felt a little grieved at the toilet things going—not razor only, but soap, tooth brush, hair brush, clean handkerchiefs, etc., were inexorably collected. I have spoken of slight discomforts, this lack of opportunity to keep oneself reasonably clean is the hardest—one wash a day, often with a sergeant fuming at one to hurry up all the time ; dirty handkerchiefs, dirty boots, dirty clothes (no clothes brush, no hair brush), dirty teeth, two days' beard—*one* towel between us (eight days for seven men so far !) and the possession of that a lucky fluke. Probably the higher officers would not approve, but we do not care to complain. Some of the guard sergeants are reasonable, and allow a book or so each, a little writing material, etc., and as the guard is changed every twenty-four hours one isn't long in the hands of those who are quite impossible. We have just been " re-allocated ". The Major was in laconic mood. " I've posted you to the 5th and 6th ———— Infantry Regiments, three to one, four to the other, stationed at Devonport. Take these men away, sergeant."

On returning to the dug-out, we found a guard ready ; corporal and three men, the stove alight, and everything merry. Three men remain in the room (it is thanks to this we get the fire), the corporal locks the door, and one poor man does sentry-go in the cold outside. Seven pacifists can cause a deal of trouble ! Two of the new guard were of the party who escorted us hither from Birmingham, and they told us some interesting details. The sergt.-major had selected his escort, paraded them, and said, " Now then, You've got some rough characters to deal with—are there any of you who have been wounded ? " Two or three fell out. " Can you deal with a rough 'ouse ? " " Yes." " All right, look after your men, sergeant, when you get there ; take your handcuffs and use them on any you think likely to give trouble ! "

Most of our men have heavy colds from our journey, from sleeping on damp "biscuits", palliasses, etc., hence the stove is primed up, all ventilation stopped—you may be sure Tommy raises no objection as the temperature steadily rises. The air is heavy with the odour of eucalyptus, and those like myself who have fortunately escaped

8

colds so far, also escape sleep. They seem getting rather stricter with us, food comes late, cold, very dirty, and sometimes short—a bucket of tea is plumped down, cold. " Two tots sunk in that," says the orderly, " drink for seven and leave for five upstairs." We fish up the " tots," and gulp cold tea whilst he waits to carry the bucket on.

When here before we had difficulty to get permission for exercise—to-day, in cold and drizzle, we have been out for two longish spells ! No visitors are allowed except relatives, so that has cut me off from two kind people who have come over to see me from Woodbrooke. Parcels are not allowed in—some have been turned back. In the guardroom proper there are five other C.O.s. They have insufficient light for writing or reading, day and night (it is almost dark all the time), and no fire, which, besides giving us heat (a good deal of it at times !) gives TOAST— and who would not find life tolerable in any circumstances, with toast ?

About the chaplain's visit. A very curt corporal suddenly came to the door and called out, " Mothers' Meeting for Conscientious Objectors — d . . . . d humbug." The other five C.O.s came down, and by and by our two visitors appeared, having been interviewing the Colonel meanwhile, we had hymns, prayer, and short addresses from our friends and were cheered and helped.

I thought I had finished this letter at last—but I find I have left out the most important thing of all. At about 10 a.m., we were taken over to the Quartermaster's stores—I knew what that meant, " Khaki ". In we went, one at a time. I came last. Quartermaster had a pile of boots on the bench before him. He handled a pair as I came in, and another sergeant said : " Now, I'm going to give you a ' legal ' order," then (trying to be very fierce, with only partial success)—" you know the serious consequences of refusal : will you put on uniform ? " " I'm sorry, sergeant : I can't comply." " All right, take him away ", and I tailed on to the others and marched back to the dug-out. So in all probability we shall be

court-martialled together here in a few days, and not have
to go to Devonport after all. Isn't it simple? *That*, at
least, we owe to the pioneer C.O.s, and they unreservedly
must have credit and gratitude.

Guard-Room, Worcester.
January 23rd, 1917.

. . . When the key of our guard room turns in the
lock, there is always a moment of excitement—little
things excite a prisoner, you know, and it may be anything
from mail to court-martial. Yesterday was quite a day of
minor thrills, all interesting in their way, but demanding
much patience, and a sound constitution if colds are to be
averted. It seems a principle to parade us on the average
about half an hour before the officer is ready to deal with
us, and we spend the time standing at attention in the
bitter cold. Yesterday we began about 10 a.m. with a
visit to the major, who, as we have seen, does not waste
words. After a long wait at the door of his office, he
suddenly came out, called over our names, said " Re-
manded ", and disappeared again. We returned to our
cellar, but had hardly settled down when we heard the
" seven prisoners up ! " again, and learned we were to
have the honour of a visit to the C.O. (not our brand).
This operation took the rest of the morning, though most
of it was spent on the icy parade ground outside his office.
When at last we entered, the proceedings were quite brief.
The two sergeants who had witnessed our disobedience on
Sunday, gave evidence, which was short and to the point,
and quickly taken down. Then the Colonel asked us
again whether we would put on khaki. When the question
came to me, I replied, " No, sir, I'm sorry to give trouble,
but I can't comply." One of us omitted the " sir ", from
a conception of principle I suppose. I confess to regretting
that some C.O.s do not try to be rather more obliging.
Some slouch and walk out of step, and with hands in
pockets ; are surly, or even commit the (to me) quite

gratuitous offence of grinning at one another in the presence of high officers—I agree the latter are just ordinary men—but it is on that account I don't like to see their— or anyone's—feelings needlessly hurt. I try to get my friends to pull themselves together, stand upright, move smartly, and I say to them, " Let's look like *men*, all the more because we are not *soldiers*." . . . Frankly, I loved the drilling in Unit preparation days. The thought of relieving suffering sanctified and inspired every action. I was playing, not for myself but for my side, which had a goal to score. I was *glad* to submit to discipline—I believe the jumping up at any hour of the day or night in obedience to an order, regardless of my own inclination or comfort, was an invaluable lesson in my life. Forgive me, I am just thinking aloud, and feel I haven't got to the bottom of this matter yet—so many of my comrades look at it differently.

Well, to return to my yarn, the Colonel looked over his specs. and said : " How do they teach you to address your own people, ' Quakers ', or whatever it is ? " No reply. " Because you're expected to address people properly here." I don't know whether he thought the Society of Friends was another sort of machine, doing a different job, but working on the same general system, as his own ! I felt sorry for the poor old man, he was so helpless just then, and knew it : but I suppose he can get his own back at the D.C.M. if he likes. I shouldn't say he'll descend to that, however—my impression is that most army officers are " gentlemen " in a sense of the term that has a not unworthy meaning. I am afraid some of us do not always appear so to them—according to their definition. A mutual understanding would remove the misapprehension —but of this there is little likelihood just now, I am afraid.

This little episode over, the Colonel relapsed into his safer brevity, simply pronouncing the words : " District Court-martial," and we filed out. After dinner there were symptoms of the big machine hustling itself. The typed copies of evidence, etc., were being already prepared, and we spent most of the afternoon as we had spent the morning, with lengthy waits and brief interviews. I found myself alone in a passage at one time, with only one guard. This guard happened to be the sergeant whose " legal order " I had disobeyed. I had a little talk with him about it, saying how I hated refusing any service, etc. He was rather moved, I think, and mumbled something about hating the business too, but having to do his duty. I felt now that there was really no cloud between me and anyone in the barracks, and was glad that this little opportunity had occurred.

When I see so many men about the barracks with one, two, three, or even more of the little vertical gold stripes on their sleeve, hobbling about on sticks, or with arms hanging useless, I hope to myself that if any C.O.s should meet with contempt or abuse in the army (which in *my* experience they don't, except from just one or two out of a hundred), they may have the grace quietly to understand. . . .

We have now been here sufficiently long to have settled down to a more or less regular routine life, except for the little alarums and excursions already referred to. One day we got a beam of sunshine through the windows, outside of which is a steep bank of rough grass and bushes, surmounted by a low wall and railings which border the road—but the bank is high and shuts out all other view, and most of the sky, but the little glimpse we get is refreshing. Heavy bars cover the window frame outside, but we can raise the window to let in an occasional cat or to throw crumbs to a fat thrush that entertains us by pulling worms out of the bank. Wouldn't all this have been sweet solace to many a poor prisoner of history whose bleak captivity one recalls ! The evening is the time we most look forward to. We hang up a blanket in front of the window, and light the gas. The burner gives only a tiny glimmer in the room, but by taking if off, we get a long yellow cylinder of smoky flame, close to which it is reasonably possibly to write. Now, sitting on blankets on the floor (there is only one little seat which can hold at most four out of the eleven of us), we play games, sing, discuss, read (though only devotional books have been permitted, not very appropriate for continuous reading aloud) or chat with the soldiers. At " first post " we have our little times of worship and a closing hymn. Then we set about preparing to turn in. Spread our blankets on the floor, take off outer garments and roost,—it is very simple converting our cellar into a bedroom. " Last post," at 10 p.m., finds every inch of floor space covered, the gas lowered, the stove giving a warm, ruddy glow. This is rather a pleasant moment, when we think especially of absent friends, and speak quietly of them. The bugle sounds "lights out", the final call of the day—the guard on duty (they sit up in watches through the night—an apology for sentry-go outside the door) puts out the gas glimmer, and now only the stove sends a fitful light over the sleepers. The music of those three last bugle calls of the day will long linger in my memory, recalling sweet moments of communion with home and friends, as I lie on my back on the hard floor. My place is next the coal box, so you may guess what happens when the guard stokes up the fire, as he does two or three times during the night, with a bit of cardboard for an improvised shovel. His big boots *try* to pick out the join between me and my neighbour, but even if he succeeds in this, I do not escape a free sprinkling of coal, which gets eventually between me and the floor !

It is good getting to know so many soldiers in the intimate way possible when one lives night and day with them in so small a compass. We have a fresh four every day and so get to know a large number. Every time we go out we meet some of these old friends about the grounds or barracks, and get a jolly smile and wag of the head. Of an evening over game and song the fraternizing is delightfully in evidence. Soldiers are *dears*, most of them. I have little doubt that the average German soldier is pretty much the same. The " Prussian war idol " is a conception that obsesses some minds ; but I am quite sure that *love of human kind* is a far greater reality, and it is through the lens of fear, ignorance and prejudice (German and English), that the one expands and the other shrinks till the true proportion is distorted as violently as we find it to-day. Does one really need to go to prison to see this? My conviction of the basic kindness of human nature has been happily strengthened by acquaintance with soldiers inside the barracks at home, just as it was by contact with them outside at the front. It is comforting to go to prison with this confirmation, for my hopes depend upon it.

Guard-Room, Worcester.
January 31st, 1917.

With the D.C.M. over, we feel that the last lap of the journey, and that a short one, has begun ; a few days hence we shall leave here *en route* for Scrubs. I think all of us will be glad—here we are not uncomfortable, and have (now we are getting known) many little privileges for which we are very thankful—but there is a feeling that we are simply waiting—detention in barracks is an interim which is neither a time of preparation, nor the test itself— the real thing that is going to try our temper, and with which we are eager to be at grips. P———, who is a Quaker visitor at certain prisons in the North, says rather a serious thing in a recent letter to me. Of all the men he has watched through gaol, he knows only one who has come forth strengthened and purified ; he does not say what the effect on character was in other cases, but I hope and think it was at least not a negative one. I feel this is a challenge to us, and we are trying to accept it as such ; it is a big adventure and we are keen to set out upon it. It sounds so funny to speak of prison as being in any sense an adventure—but, it really is when thought of in the light of that challenge—much more so than going out to the front ; for example, the dangers are so much subtler, more insidious, incalculable. The equipment must be so entirely spiritual ; no material resources will avail in this

lone struggle. It is the spiritual adventure we have so
often spoken of, the naked duel between human weakness
and divine strength in a man, with no hope of reinforce-
ments from any of the allies that help in everyday life—
Nature, freedom, the congenial task, human fellowship,
communal worship, little physical comforts and the like.
It is a trial alone in the desert, and if one dwells on past
defeats in this kind of warfare, one has moments of something like fear. But spiritual fellowship with friends there
will be—and I want to say that the experience of three
weeks' detention has been nothing less than a revelation—
a new wonderful revelation of the help that this may be to
one. This with loving gratitude to all who have surrounded me with thoughts and prayer at this time. Without that, the issue of the conflict would be less sure. There
is really little to say about the court-martial ; it was all so
quiet and simple and straightforward. Since being
officially " warned " on Sunday, our thought had naturally
been turning a good deal towards it, and there was much
traffic with pencils and paper in preparing statements.
In the evening, at our little time of fellowship, we prayed
that if the day should bring us into opposition with any,
we might be kept in a spirit of love for all, remembering
it is for that we are here.

Early morning saw us all making brave efforts with our
meagre toilet equipment—unprecedented attempts at
cleanliness in spite of difficulties. A kind corporal lent us
boot-cleaning equipment, but no clothes brush could be
obtained, and I saw the boot polisher doing duty in some
cases, with questionable results I am afraid. . . . Our
guards were amused and interested in the proceedings,
and declared we could not have taken more care if we had
been titifying for a party. In result, I felt dreadfully like
a whited sepulchre, and would not have had mother see
my shirt for a good deal !

TRIAL BY DISTRICT
COURT-MARTIAL

THE day began early : immediately after breakfast we were taken to see the Doctor again—marched up and down for about an hour outside the hospital in bitter cold waiting for him, and were eventually in his office about two minutes. He just said, " Any who refuse medical examination put their hands up." It was a case of " carried unanimously ", or " The noes have it "—we were marched out again, having been " deemed " fit to stand the strain of D.C.M. It is quite simple really, being " deemed " to be things, from a soldier downwards through all that it implies ; I am not sure, however, that it would be a desirable principle to introduce widely into everyday life. I hope the Government's little experiment with it will convince them of that. I think it might make rather a good game for children ! As soon as we had been duly deemed by the doctor, we were taken to the awe-inspiring building where the Court was to be held, and, after another wait, ushered into the Presence. The room was a long, clean, pleasant one, the barracks' library. I did not notice many details of it except that the number of books was exiguous, and that there was a large portrait on the wall, at about the spot where my eyes happened to focus, when later on I was standing at my trial. I remember every minute detail of that old, discoloured print, but practically nothing else. I was last on the list and did not get tried until about 3.30 p.m. I felt a wonderful sense of confidence and of having a message to give. When the time came I read it quietly and without any feeling of nervousness. The officers were all extremely courteous, and one had a feeling that they honestly desired to dispense justice according to the rules of the game.

I pleaded " technically guilty ", and when the President
said he understood my meaning, but that he was bound
to make it either " guilty " or " not guilty", I said I did
not wish to give any unnecessary trouble (it makes the
proceedings longer to plead " not guilty "), and was
willing to plead " guilty " so far as that court was concerned. He said, " Oh, you're not giving any trouble ",
and almost pressed me to plead " not guilty ", from an
excessive sense of fairness, I apprehend. However, I
persisted in being guilty, and things went ahead. Afterwards my friends walked back across the barrack yard
with me, transferring chocolate, etc., to my pockets, and
finally I waved them good-bye at the gates, as I disappeared into the dug-out, where, to my joy, I found my
comrades already assembled. That sense of deep gladness
and spiritual inspiration which had upheld me in the
Court made us so happy that it seemed—so I said to myself
—like a foretaste of the millenium, whatever that is. In
the evening, when we had spread our blankets and lay on
our backs, thinking of the day and of friends, before
turning over to go to sleep, it was like our first Police cells
night for glory !

On Sunday we shall be " read out " before the whole
company assembled—i.e., the sentences, having been duly
confirmed by the War Office, will be read to us by the
Colonel, and on Monday we shall leave for the Scrubs.

Guard-Room, ——— Barracks,
Worcester.

February 1st, 1917.

As the period of our detention in barracks draws rapidly
to a close, one becomes more and more inclined to look
kindly upon it, dwelling upon the little humours and
amenities that redeem the trials and discomforts in every
phase of life that I have yet experienced—at any rate in
after-thought. The early days in Belgium come back
constantly to my mind, brought there no doubt by hard

floors at night, coarse food (eaten with improvised tools), sleeping in one's clothes, and the like ; but no doubt above all by thrashing out many an incident of those thrilling times with soldier-guards who were in the same neighbourhood. Roads, houses, *estaminets*, *chateaux*, that country is familiar as one's native heath to all who have been there ; chatting of incidents which cling around many of those places, one often hears, " Oh that old *chateau* is in ruins now, they began shelling it at such and such a time." " Yes, I know that *estaminet*, our company was halting there once when they dropped a shell in the yard and pegged eleven of our men," and so on.   I forget what I was going to say ! Oh, I remember—that the fun one got out of the discomforts (which were many) of those days, is the chief thing one remembers about them—or at least the rest dissolves in retrospect.   Here in our little dug-out, where by the time we leave on Monday next, we shall have lived for three weeks, it is just the same.   One of the things I shall never forget is the extraordinary good nature of the corporals in charge.   The men have been different each day, but after a run of five corporals, the series began again, like a recurring decimal ; their movements are evidently periodic, so we have got to know them even better than the men.   One thinks, and will think, of the five of them with real affection, finding it difficult to say which one likes most ; and I think being glad to leave it open in appreciation of the way in which kind-heartedness is tinged and varied by personality, and is all the more good to experience on that account.   Among the guards we have had some real character studies—one could sit all day listening to their prattle.   The soldier at least learns the art of conversation, light banter and repartee.   Then of course the tales of the front are always intensely interesting, and any group of soldiers invariably comes to trench gossip before long.   The things they talk about in the most casual way as they sit round the stove pulling contentedly at their old pipes simply astound one ; these simple, kind, profane men are using terms never before heard, to describe

scenes never before acted in the whole history of the world—
they are so unconsciously graphic ; illustrated papers,
films, the most vivid written descriptions, pale beside these
colour-photograph kaleidoscopic *viva voce* views. It's a
mystery to me *how* the kind hearts persist through all that
they've seen and *done*—upsets some of my theories a little—
but one is thankful for it.   They've nearly all been wounded
on the Somme—it's rare to meet a man wounded anywhere else—the latest wound, at least.   The horror of it
doesn't come home to them, I am convinced of that.   The
hardening process must be far more rapid than I thought.
Hear boys of eighteen talk of going over the parapets at
night—creeping across no man's land, every now and then
putting a hand on a dead man's face—sometimes mis-
taking it for a German creeping in the opposite direction,
and lying dead still for a moment beside the corpse for fear
of a row—or clubbing it in sudden frenzy, and much more
in incredible variety of ghastliness, all told over toast and
bully beef around the stove, as naturally as football gossip
used to be purveyed in earlier times.   About the barracks
are men who have been shot through the head, and go
raving mad every now and again, or just quietly silly so
that men laugh at them.   How it recalls long nights by
the bedsides of poor raving *poilus—pères de famille* in hospital
and ambulance at the front !—nothing moved me more
to hot indignation against war.   When I think of the
hardening process in my own case, despite the nature of my
work,—its rich measure of inspiration—I need hardly
wonder perhaps, that it is terribly rapid when the work is
so different.   But if the sense of horror passes men by
without moving them, that of utter weariness, of the utter
futility of it all, certainly does *not*.   I had heard stories
of the attitude of mind of men at the front, had read an
illuminating letter or two—but the *universality*, the *force* of
the sentiment has been a startling revelation.   We've had
about sixty guards so far, with whom we have lived, slept,
eaten (and let me recommend life in a cellar with locked
door and a stove for really getting to know people)—not

one who is not only sick to death of the war, but wholly disillusioned of all the lying tricks and deceptions by which it becomes possible to set normal human beings at slaughtering each other. All the most popular songs in the army now express this ennui, and are sung with entire impunity. One of them begins :

> " I don't want to go to the trenches again ;
> Oh, my ! I don't want to die."

I've forgotten the rest.   .   .   .   I heard it first in the open street at Birmingham, sung by a company marching to the station en route for the Front. The sight of them and the words of that second line, hit me with overwhelming pathos—girls, women and children were running alongside, some in tears. I've heard it sung so often since then lightheartedly, that the sense of pathos has gone out— but I remember what it was that first time. Of course we meet hundreds of soldiers about the barracks on little odd occasions, when there are moments of chat only less intimate than with our own guards. We'd been here ten days before we met a man who did not completely concede the position we took up—then a fat old ex-Adult School man showed a tendency to argue on the usual civilian lines, but very soon lapsed into silence. The Adult School touch, by the way, is rather interesting. I think it revealed a state of mental uneasiness, and a feeling of the necessity for self-justification. I only remember two others who put up any case, and both these gave up and became the best of pals. A few—very few—say they would volunteer if the war broke out again, but they are wholly sympathetic with us at the same time. On the eve of our court-martial, one young fellow, better educated than most we have had to do with, called us quietly aside into the passage, with a sort of " concern " which he expressed, obviously affected— wished us the best of luck, said he believed every man ought to follow the dictates of conscience, etc. But most of them, less educated, are much more outspoken.

It does my heart good—I, who have been so deeply

distressed by the tone of the newspapers since my return from France—to hear the soldiers reading them with running comment. " If those newspaper blokes that go to the front would ask the fellows in the trenches straight, they'd hear a different story." Reading a picture paper account of Silvertown,* where soldiers are depicted clearing away *débris* " with great energy, but showing clearly their eagerness to be at grips with the enemy "—chorus : " I don't think." A few of the sergeants are very sharp— but I was told by one man that the men who call C.O.s cowards are often just the ones who have shown the white feather at the front—" gone sick " when there is bombing party work on hand, etc. But anyway the jeering N.C.O.s are a very small minority—offset by many others who address a C.O. as " Sir ", or a group as " gentlemen "— quite gratuitous politeness. When in the presence of an officer it has to be " private ", but never on other occasions —it is " Mr." then. A parcel came down the other day, announced as for " Private—beg pardon, Mr. So-and-So."

We have had some rummy guards—one, a half-witted boy of twenty, terrible stoop, almost a deformity, sits all day mouth open, eyes half closed, pale as a ghost, never speaks a word, he goes by the name of " Dead 'un " in the barracks, and when the soldiers meet him they call out : " They've opened another box " (coffin), pointing at him. Poor Sammy, a half-baked Devonshire dumpling, is another joke of the barracks—perpetually having his leg pulled, taking it in the best of humour, enjoying thoroughly the jokes at his own expense—talking the whole day long in broadest accent, really funny, and quite a favourite amongst us. But " Dead 'un " is tragedy, not comedy.

This last week many little amenities have softened our lot ; after a fortnight's detention we had the good fortune to have our old grand-motherly sergeant as chief of the guard. In our recent tour of the home counties under his superintendence we had established a certain authority

* Where a Munitions Factory explosion had occurred.

over him by reason of his dependence upon us for remembering his documents, catching trains, and most principally, not losing ourselves ! Thanks to this moral ascendancy, we were able to raid our kits and get almost anything we wanted—toilet things and books were the greatest *desiderata* —and since then I have been enjoying *Browning as a Philosophical and Religious Teacher*. I hope to finish this and then do *Sartor* again, so as to take Browning's and Carlyle's philosophies of life with me to think over during Scrubs months. Letters and parcels have come in thick and fast, too—both containing good things. I have been specially and undeservedly favoured. I admired so much the entire absence of jealousy on the part of the others, who were longing for letters. I shared all mine that lent themselves to sharing, which many fortunately did. " Who's Catchpool ? " said the orderly coming in one morning a day or two ago, and then : " Christ, there's enough letters to keep you going for a month ! " Those that travelled round the country after us, and had to be forwarded from barracks to barracks, were mostly adorned with uncomplimentary remarks on the back *a propos* conscientious objectors.

But what has also meant very much indeed to me has been the half-hour's exercise we have been able to get fairly regularly morning and afternoon of late—not the fresh air and physical benefit alone (I won considerable *kudos* in the barracks by running the whole half-hour, covering nearly six miles on one occasion !) but the glimpses of country which one snapshots and takes back into detention (and will carry into the little cells yonder). At the end of the parade ground is a wide gate, through which one gets an exquisite peep at the Cathedral over a jumble of red-tiled roofs—a distant foreground, with the Clee Hills full-back, chequered with the snow which lies deep in the rifts. Mists from the Severn veil the Cathedral in white vapour ; but often it breaks through, or the sudden sun picks it out from the rest, clean and white above the smoke. At dawn, when we go up to wash after reveillé at 6.30, one gets lovely effects. Then there is always the sky, even when our glimpse of the big world is hidden, and I have discovered how much I love the sky. I think it means more to me than any other feature of nature. Since snow has been lying on the ground these last few days we have had periods of bright sunshine and lovely cloud effects. What compensations we have for what Southrons call our abominable climate ! I have longed since the day we came from Birmingham three weeks ago (when everything was blotted out by drizzling rain), for a sight of the Malverns. It has been so tantalizing to know that wonderful contour against the sky so near, and yet to miss it. For in spite of several ruses I have not succeeded. I had the hope partly in mind when trying to get permission to go to Church on Sunday, but learned that " prisoners lose all those *privileges* ". I remembered a story heard a day or two before, of a company being marched four miles in the baking sun with full kit and *outfit of bombs* to a twenty minutes' service—and comments on the proceeding !

The birds—starlings, blackbirds, finches, sparrows, wagtails, robins and tits, that had got to know where a supply of crumbs is to be had this frosty weather, have been another constant delight. If we forget to throw them out, a robin—bolder than his bigger brethren—is sent up as a deputation, perches on the iron bars just beyond the panes, and cocks his old head on one side in irresistible fashion.

In spite of so much to distract, there have been signs of growing restlessness amongst us—loss of liberty *does* tell. Well, comfort and discomfort—privation and amenity— it's all at an end now. At 2.15 p.m. to-day, we were suddenly and unexpectedly paraded and " read out ". The barracks was paraded too, there were not many in at the moment, about 100 men. The Adjutant read out our sentences one by one—112 days hard labour in each case—and we stood forward in turn before the assembled company. Half of them were old guard-room pals, and most certainly were feeling sympathetic ; many gave as noticeable a wag of the head and grin as they dared under the severe eye of the regimental sergeant-major. Immediately it was over the N.C.O. in charge of us prisoners came up close and said *sotto voce* : " Well, good luck, chaps." We marched down to Shrub Hill, sent wires, violently wrote post cards till the train came in, and are now *en route* for Scrubs. Heigho ! now for the sustained tussle. As I go to it, two thoughts are uppermost in my mind—first the revelation of the kindness of all our friends, from that tiring whole day's wait of some of them at the recruiting office, through all the loving messages of detention days, to the promise of surrounding thought and prayer in our coming loneliness—and next, the goodness of human hearts everywhere, from the big motherly wardress at the lock-up, who had four sons in the trenches, but could yet call a posse of C.O.s "my boys", throughout the barracks *personnel* to our present escort, old friends who rejoice in their success in the competition to accompany us. (Honesty compels me to say that this is not entirely unconnected with prospects of backsheesh !) But anyway, barracks, which used to stand to me for the antithesis of home and all implied by it, had quite a quaint little homely feeling to impart as I left them to-day—why ? Because it's human beings, not bricks and mortar that make even a barracks, and humans are good and kind.

EDITOR'S NOTE.—On arrival at Paddington the prisoners and their guard were met by a group of relatives and friends. The whole company repaired to a neighbouring restaurant to spend a brief hour in fellowship and to share a " last supper " before the long separation. The little band then went on to Wormwood Scrubs. Referring to the warmth of feeling expressed by the guard when they bid them farewell at the great gate of the prison, C.C. says, " I shall long remember the genuine handgrip, the few kind words of cheer, supplemented in one case by a whisper, the very last words I heard before going in, ' There's hardly a man in barracks but honours you in his heart.' "

Letters are allowed to be written and received by prisoners at rare intervals, but the regulations are framed to restrict the correspondence in the main to private and personal matters.

In the early days of May 1917, C.C. was released from Wormwood Scrubs prison and taken under escort to Devonport. Early next day the " legal " order was given and on stating that, without any disrespect to the officer and regretting to cause trouble, his conscientious convictions would not allow him to comply, C.C. was again put under arrest, and shortly after he was confined in a detention cell to await a second trial by court-martial. The following is a brief outline of the D.C.M. proceedings, together with his statement to the Court :

DISTRICT COURT-MARTIAL No. 2

Devonport.

May 12th, 1917.

10 a.m.

ASKED if he had anything to say in mitigation C.C. replied that in explanation, rather than with a view to mitigation, he wished to read a *Statement* (as follows) :—

" In explanation of my presence before this Court I wish to offer a brief statement of my faith, and of the duty it has laid upon me.

" I look upon the *whole* of life as a sacrament of service, demanding loyalty to the highest ideal. For me, this ideal is the life of Jesus Christ. In the light of His teaching, I regard no man as my enemy, and am convinced of the wrongfulness of all war. If I am met with gas, bombs and bayonets, I will not poison and kill in return. I believe there is a heroism other than that which involves the infliction of pain and death : a surer protection for those I love than the slaughter of those whom someone else loves. With God's help I will make the great adventure of faith, standing fearless, unweaponed save with the power of redemptive love. I have an unfaltering faith in human nature, and seek no protection but that which God wills for those who trust Him. This is my understanding of Christ's way of life, a *practical* way, both for individuals and for nations ; the only way that can rid the world of war. Some day a nation will have the courage to disarm, and put these convictions to the test ; and I have absolute confidence in the issue. Meanwhile, believing that moral progress comes through individual faithfulness to ideals, I am trying, though very conscious of failure and inconsistency, to be loyal to them in my own life.

" On the outbreak of war there was great need of ambulance workers. I could not join the army even for this

service ; but I immediately left my profession and qualified
for Red Cross work. After a few weeks' training, I offered
myself for voluntary service on the battlefield, with a little
Ambulance Unit organized by a few young Quakers, the
religious body to which I have belonged since childhood.
We went out to the Ypres sector when the fate of Flanders
still hung in the balance. I little expected ever to return,
and asked only the privilege of serving, for a few weeks at
least, in saving life. I went out longing to relieve the
suffering caused by war, to show sympathy with men who
had obeyed a call of duty different from my own, and, in
a labour of love, to share the dangers and hardships to
which they were exposed. For nineteen months I was
spared to continue this work at the front. Meanwhile,
however, the medical service had become completely
organized. Voluntary units were either dispensed with,
or practically absorbed into the regular armies. The
wounded no longer lacked help, the R.A.M.C. being often
closed to applicants. Men displaced by the services taken
over by the Unit, of which I had become Adjutant, were
often drafted to the firing line, and complained bitterly that
I and my colleagues had sent them there.

" I was baffled more and more by the consciousness that,
under military control, the primary object of our work
was the refitting of men to take their place again in the
trenches. Conscription followed, and it seemed to me
that, for one called to serve in the cause of peace, the position
was becoming impossible. At home, men who stood for
the same ideals as myself were being reviled as cowards
and shirkers, and forced into the army against their
principles. When some of them were sent to France and
became liable to the death penalty, I hesitated no longer.
It seemed to me more honest and more manly to take my
stand with them, make public profession of my faith, and
accept the consequences.

" I could have obtained exemption by continuing
ambulance work, had I felt it right to do so ; I was begged
to secure it by undertaking some ' alternative service '

recognized as 'important' in organization for war. But I am enlisted in the highest service I know, the formation of a world-fellowship of men prepared to die rather than take part in war ; and the foundations of such a fellowship, which is already spreading from country to country, cannot rest upon compromise.

"I went before the tribunals, but was refused the absolute exemption provided by the Act for genuine cases. I was committed to prison, and have just finished a sentence of 112 days hard labour in the third division. I have many friends in the army. I admire their courage : I understand and honour their obedience to duty. I believe that the hardest course a strong young man, eager for service, could be called upon to follow at a time like the present, is to stand aside and withhold from sharing their sublime self-sacrifice. I ask the officers before whom I stand to believe me that it is so in my own experience, and that only a supreme sense of duty enables me to take this course. The spectacle before the world to-day of two great nations slaughtering each other's manhood, starving each other's women and children, strengthens my faith in the better way of life which I have outlined, and lays upon me afresh the duty of proclaiming it."

IN GUARD-ROOM AT DEVONPORT

Devonport.
May 10th, 1917.

IT has been a great blow to me, on coming out again after three-and-a-half months, to find the war clouds still so black, to scan the horizon with so little trace of dawn. One is apt to expect too much to have happened during the prison blank, and there is disappointment in finding the situation much the same, if not even darker. Cut off from all except the baldest outline of facts, one weaves into them grotesque patterns which prove to be far from the truth. It reminds me of the game we used to play of drawing pigs blindfold—only the pigs one draws in Scrubs are better than nature, whilst it is the other way round in the nursery game ! I have been so cheery and optimistic all the time in prison, but I confess to feeling a shade depressed on coming out ! Day by day I have poured out my soul in prayer for peace. You know it is not myself I am thinking of. The anguish of the world gives me continuous heart-ache. I have often felt that I would gladly endure the worse-than-death of a life sentence in prison, if so I could help free the world from the bonds of fear.

It must be hard to go steadily on with one's regular work during these dark days—I can well believe it is harder than prison or the trenches. I fancy I should put the order thus, for myself, hardest of all, to go on normally— next, prison—least hard (assuming a quiet conscience), the trenches.

Devonport.
May 14th, 1917.

Here we go on quietly as usual, and there is very little to report. Our exercise ground was so blocked up with straw to-day that we were allowed to walk up and down outside instead. Two out of a large number of men who were drilling, whispered, " Stick it boys ! " An officer who noticed us sent the sergt.-major a little later on, and had us marched back (not discourteously) to our little pitch, in spite of the straw. They are positively afraid of even our silent influence upon the men.

After the D.C.M., Lieut. ⸻, whose order I had refused, called me aside and invited me to speak of my views. He was most pleasant, broad-minded, and genuinely desiring to understand, I think. " If you knew what it was to be in a tight place in the trenches," he said, " when an extra man or two might have made all the difference, you would understand why we want you in the army ! " That let in light for me on his difficulty, " It is just this," he continued, " the side with most men and guns wins."

How can one talk to the army about *spiritual influence*, which is at the bottom of everything for me ? Lieut. ⸻ was, I am sure, a man who cares that righteousness prevail, yet it had never occurred to him that the side with most guns wasn't necessarily the side most right.

I am in no hurry to get to prison. I dread it a good deal in prospect, but am confident that, once embarked upon it, I shall come through as quietly and calmly as before.

The papers fascinate me—it is like coming out of a dark cellar into dazzling light (simile not a good one, in view of the present world obscurity !) which attracts and yet hurts. To me, to be shut off from news of the world is like being in ignorance of the welfare of a loved one, always worse than knowledge, even if the news be bad. As I was saying to-day, I seem hardly able even to pray intelligently unless I *know*.

One of the sergeants died very suddenly to-day of heart failure, and they are getting up a subscription for a wreath. I heard about it, and asked if I might subscribe 2s. They accepted gladly, and my name will be posted up with the list of other subscribers, rather unusual for a prisoner just court-martialled, I imagine !

You must not expect the influencing of D.C.M. by any statement that could be made at it. The kind of statement we make cannot possibly affect the decision, though it may affect the man, who—even in a Prussian, " *Loytnant* " is implicit in the soldier. The D.C.M. simply has to consider the question of military law—Was or was not a military order disobeyed, and what is a meet punishment ? As the prosecutor reminded the Court, religion is expressly stated in Manual of Military Law to provide no excuse for dereliction of military duty. Once inside the army, conscience does not exist. No one would be more thankful than I for unconditional release, and God knows that the desire for service has never burned with a purer flame within me—but it cannot come from a D.C.M.—we must put that out of our minds. I think on the other hand that the conscience of many has been really stirred to shame by Russia, and it is just conceivable, I think, that Russia may yet set us free. It would, however, be the greatest mistake to build upon it—we may have very many months of prison before us yet. And we are all agreed that any move to ease our lot or further divide our ranks, without the victory we are waiting for, would be worse than useless —dangerous to the Cause.

SENTENCED AGAIN—
"TWELVE MONTHS' HARD LABOUR"

Devonport.
May 16th, 1917.

WE were " read out " this morning. I came first, two years hard labour, commuted to one year hard labour " in recognition of services in ambulance work ". You will remember that I said I did not make my statement with a view to mitigation, but in explanation. However, it appears to have " mitigated " none the less, and my only anxiety is lest that in doing so it failed to " explain ".

I would rather have shared the fate of my colleagues, but it makes no practical difference, as most second sentences seem to be commuted to six months now. I believe the authorities think that by these repeated passages through the barrack guard-room and C.M. business, they provide themselves with a series of chances of breaking us down and roping us into the army. It strikes one as being a curious comment on the " coward and shirker " cry of Tribunals, that only when a man's courage and determination has been thoroughly broken do they come down to the ordinary " hero's " level, and start upon a military career !

A new officer has been censoring our letters the last two days. I fancy the C.O. gave orders that they were to be much more strict. He seems needlessly and brutally inquisitive, asking as he looks at the signatures, " Who's this fellow ? " " Who's so-and-so ? " " What woman's this, your sweetheart ? " and so on, reading through every word of the letters, and laying down his dictum, " Nothing connected with your beliefs, peace, your position here, etc. "—I hardly know what he expects one's friends to write about. After remarking over ———'s innocent

'letter, " I wish to —— they wouldn't write this stuff,"
he did, to be sure, volunteer a suggestion, " They can say
they're damned sorry for you, you know, and all that."
I hastily assured him they weren't !

The sergeant who was at the D.C.M. came up yesterday,
and said he had listened to all I said, and respected my
principles. He seemed quite affected, and asked for our
address in London, saying he was a Londoner, and should
write to you, or go to see you when he had his leave !

Reverting to the censoring, when a big packet of type-
written stuff was condemned, I begged leave at least to
be allowed to return it unread. As an envelope was en-
closed for return of the documents, I thought there might
be no copy and that they might be valuable. The sergeant
who was present, saw the point, and suggested several times
that the best thing would be to put them all in the envelope
and send them back. But the only response was slowly to
tear them up ! His excuse was that it was against D.O.R.A.
What are we coming to when young subalterns take upon
themselves to be administrators and judges of civil law ?

Guard Room, —— Barracks.
May 17th, 1917.

This is my penultimate epistle—we hear this evening
that we are to leave for Exeter Goal at 9.30 a.m. to-morrow,
under escort of a sergeant and two men. The officer who
has been censoring our letters the last few days—of which
process more anon—has just been up and taken every shred
of anything of value from us : money, stamps, pocket
knives, watches, wedding rings, etc. I don't know whether
such a proceeding is legal. The officer is autocrat enough,
I fancy, to invent any regulation that he thought would
help reduce us to a due realization of our state of serfdom
and impotence—e.g., I haven't a half-penny left to buy a
paper in the morning, and we shall either have to hustle
into prison before 12 (if possible), or else go without a
midday meal. However, the little scheme for humiliating

us did not work quite so perfectly in all its details as may have been wished. It did not occur to him, probably, that fortune could favour the conscientious objector (I think it would shake his belief in providence if he knew it had done!) However, my turn came last, and I had overheard enough to gather what was afoot. Earlier in the day, at exercise, we had whipped round for a tip to our sergeant, which had been entrusted to me for handing over. So the first thing I did was to pop out and hand it to him on the quiet. Next I made a hasty list of all the folks I wanted to write a farewell letter or post card to—I had about half a dozen penny and several half-penny stamps left. These I clapped quickly on to envelopes and cards, addressed them, and laid them in a pile on my table. When asked for my stamps I said those were all I had, and he, thinking they were ready for post, let them go—hence this letter to you, and thus I saved my stamps! Then immediately the officer had gone, sergeant came along and begged me to have the money back. I told him I was not such an expert trickster as he gave me credit for and had given him the tip quite ingenuously. Well, he said, I owe you two shillings, anyway and I remembered a forgotten loan to him of a few days ago. I told him I really didn't want that back either, but felt free to ask him to post a parcel to you, and, more important (with a little spice of wickedness, and therefore of enjoyment about it), to supply us with newspapers in the morning—both of which he gladly promised to do!

We all feel (and, I think, look) very much fitter than when we came out of Scrubs. It is satisfactory to find that one seems to pick up again so readily. The army diet is much fuller than prison—nearly four times as much bread, I should say. In one respect, however, it suits me less well—viz., the large quantity of meat. I expect it's a first-class diet for fighters, but does not well suit a pacifist ex-vegetarian.

I anticipate the cells and general accommodation will be less convenient than at Scrubs. One thing I greatly hope, viz., that I may get a view. Though liable to the whole series of little punishments which I got at Scrubs, for whispering, if caught looking out of the window, it is such an inestimable boon that it is well worth the risk. The library I expect will be much poorer. The food I believe is uniform throughout all prisons—but the cooking varies a good deal, and will probably be inferior provincially. If we get there in time for dinner to-morrow, it will be " beans in candlefat " that ———— mentions in his pamphlet " 112 days Hard Labour ! "

The censoring here has become such an unpleasant occasion as almost to take away the joy of receiving letters —chiefest of guard-room amenities. The new officer brings up another with him to share the fun—reads carefully and slowly through every word, making obnoxious little noises or verbal comments *and then passes it on to his colleague*—a side-light on the phrase " an officer and a gentleman ". He makes a sheep and a goat pile. The latter he slowly and wrathfully tears up into little pieces, and then seems to look about for something to wipe his fingers on ! I had a stiff time over a batch from Woodbrooke to-day. They happened to include letters from a Russian, a Korean, and a Zulu, as luck would have it. You can imagine his inquisitiveness, having the time of his life browsing on such a crop ! It began with my Russian friend (who, as you know, labours under a German cognomen), and when I gave his nationality I was quite evidently suspected of lying. When the Korean and Zulu followed on, my reputation as some dreadful international Nihilist was settled beyond recall ! Then the same post brought a communication on the international aspect of our cause, with a quotation in Italian. The situation was just saved by the letter I was expecting from my real German friend—*not* turning up.

Nevertheless, I began to feel that it would be comfortable to leave Devonport and begin life again in prison, forgetting my evil past, and trying to be a reformed character in my new (and reformatory ?) surroundings.

Our kind N.C.O.s let us have one-and-a-half hours'
exercise this afternoon to finish up our " freedom " with.
The poor men can hardly stand the hour's wait whilst we
pace up and down—they get so restless—they could not
possibly stand prison, and one wonders what they will do
after the war.

To-morrow we shall enjoy to the full our journey over
Dartmoor and by the cliffs and sea. Could a journey to
prison be better chosen? And I shall be taking a " tender
last farewell", as the hymn says, of world news. I think
I shall go in with a little more hope than I have yet realized,
but oh, it is hard to be cut off. Well, there is hope beyond
the bubbles of earth ; but I love the poor world—suffer
with it ; and would fain be able to suffer with it, pray for
it, intelligently. I almost felt on coming out of Scrubs
that faith had been tricked by ignorance. But I have
become wiser, and shall not make the same mistake again.
Tell everyone how cheery and strong I feel—yet how I
yearn for Peace.

EDITOR'S NOTE.—C.C. was released from Exeter Prison
on Saturday, October 13th. He was taken under military
escort direct to the station en route for Harwich, whither
the battalion to which he is attached, had moved. Writing
from there a few days later, he said :

Harwich.
October 15th, 1917.

The Army is really overwhelming me with kindness.
Two officers—just the two who seemed cads at Devonport
(our censoring friend and another) have gone out of their
way to be courteous—why is it ? They are all such fine,
handsome young men, in their smart uniforms—one just
longs to be able to establish sympathetic touch at some
point with them, and when I think I am just blocking all
they are out for, like sand in the most delicate parts of their
great machine, and I feel something like humiliated at my
unworthiness, and am flung back on the thought that only

a whole life of devoted self-sacrifice can square the account, or rather, the second half of a life ! And then I shall just go back to business and happiness and security, economic and physical—and men are lying wounded for days in water-logged shell-holes.   God forgive me and help me.

"We, too, are young, we have heard the call which led
You to the conflict, heard it yearningly
The hazard and the camaraderie,
Strife, and the path of freedom, living or dead."

HORACE SHIPP.

D.C.M. No. 3

EDITOR'S NOTE.—On October 18th, 1917, six days after his release from Exeter C.C. was again called upon to answer for his faith before a District Court-martial. He did so in the following words :

" Though technically charged with disobeying a military order, my real offence is that I hold religious and moral convictions which render every act of participation in war, direct or indirect, incompatible with my sense of loyalty to God. I am a life-long member of the Society of Friends —called Quakers—who, ever since they were a people, have borne consistent testimony against all war ; and for seven years a member of the Independent Labour Party, which in the political sphere has steadfastly upheld the banner of international peace and goodwill amongst men.

" Owing to the circumstances of the war, I find myself deemed to be a soldier, and am thrust into the army. To forsake or compromise my principles just when they become difficult and unpopular would be unworthy ; but unless I do so, I cannot become a soldier in fact, whatever I may be deemed. Remaining true to them, I have already been court-martialled twice, and sentenced to 112 days' and six months' H.L. respectively in the third division. On the second occasion, after I had made my defence, I was informed by the Prosecutor that under army law, no consideration could be given by the Court to religious convictions. This being so, I am afraid that the proceedings become merely formal, and the verdict almost foregone. Do not think that I complain of any injustice on the part of courts-martial, we are all in the meshes of circumstances which we had little or no hand in shaping. I daresay the army finds it just as uncomfortable to have ' deemed soldiers ' like myself to deal with, as we find it to be in the army. Yet I have met with unfailing courtesy at my trials. I know that this Court has to administer army law, and in that sense, I admit myself guilty, and have pleaded accordingly. Indeed, one reason why I am called a ' conscientious objector ' is that I must always put first as a motive for conduct those religious convictions of which the army can make no recognition. It will be said that, in any community, small minorities must sometimes suffer, and I agree. But I believe that it is an axiom of good government that they should, as far as possible, receive protection. This, surely, was the purpose of the exemption clauses in the Military Service Acts. Several forms of exemption were provided, including absolute. exemption on the grounds of religious or moral objection to war. In my first application, made more than two-and-a-half years ago, I stated that merely qualified or conditional exemption would be a violation of my convictions, and that I therefore claimed *absolute* exemption from the provisions of the Act. From this position I have never wavered. The claim was granted ; but six months after, my certificate of absolute exemption was cancelled, unfairly as I think, in circumstances that I need not detail here.

" I believe that England will be honoured in history for having had the courage to introduce exemptions on conscientious grounds—had she not done so, some thousands of us would have been shot, a fate which overtook many under the less liberal *régimes* of Germany, Russia and Austria. But I believe the order to shoot would have been repugnant to the British army, and to large sections of our people. The machinery of the Act, though designed with good intentions, often broke down in working, and owing to this and the inherent difficulties of the situation, much confusion has resulted. I cannot blame anyone, in circumstances that have been trying for all : but in view of the generous spirit manifested, and the unpleasant necessity avoided, by the offer of exemption, it seems hardly consistent with essential justice to imprison repeatedly, and for what is virtually the same offence, the men who may properly claim it.

" I believe that none of the three civil Tribunals before which I appeared had any doubt of my sincerity ; and I have reason to think that they did not give full weight to the provisions of the Act which entitled them to grant me absolute exemption. I therefore ask the Court to refer my case back to them for re-hearing, the more especially as these Tribunals were set up specifically to investigate those religious and moral convictions to which the present enquiry can give no consideration. . . . If, however, I must return to prison, I go forward in quietness and confidence ; for these convictions, though I may not explain them now, are no mere negatives—rather, a strong positive faith in a practical alternative to the way of war, and in the ultimate triumph of the cause of Peace, for which I witness to-day. We conscientious objectors are often called cowards and shirkers : but at least we are not renegades. Loyalty to principle prevents us from expressing loyalty to country in the same way as the soldier, but I dare to hope, none the less, that we are still patriots.

"Realizing that I may be shut away again from the world and from active forms of service for months, or even years, in the appalling silence of a prison cell, I have a wistful desire at least not to go there feeling that we conscientious objectors are misunderstood. We often long for a call to some work of danger and hardships, like those that our brave soldiers are facing with sublime self-sacrifice in the trenches. But should no such chance be offered us, will you not respect a man who keeps steadily on in what he believes to be the line of duty, rather than turn aside merely to remove unjust suspicion, or demonstrate that he, too, can dare and suffer ?

" I find that it sometimes helps to explain the spirit of our cause if I tell people that, on the outbreak of war, I went to the front for voluntary ambulance work, and served for nineteen months in the danger zone in Flanders. I mention it now solely for that purpose ; for it would have been far harder for me to have stayed at home, and I know that it *was* harder for many of my friends whose

10

duty led them to remain. When we are called shirkers—men who refuse to serve their country—my thoughts sometimes go back to an occasion many years ago, at a Quaker school in the North of England, when I, and others who are in prison to-day, thrilled as our Headmaster put before us ideals of service and citizenship in the great world we were about to enter. Though faltering often, we have striven to keep those ideals before us, and their realization is still the purpose of our effort. If taunted that we have not enlisted for three years or the duration of war, we can only reply that we have enlisted for life. And if it is said that our path of service is at least safe, I suggest that it is not necessarily easier thereby for a *young man* to follow.

" Two and a half centuries ago our Quaker ancestors were filling the dungeons of this land, dying often of exhaustion in prison before they reached the age of thirty, giving their young lives in the cause of religious freedom. Much for which they suffered has perished in the storm of war, and the world has hardly realized its loss.

" We are suffering imprisonment to-day, and are prepared to suffer death, as they did, not only to salvage these shipwrecked liberties, but to help in shaping a new world from which the dark clouds of war shall have rolled away for ever, and in which this precious heritage of the past may be handed down, an inviolable possession, to generations yet unborn."

Harwich.

October 20th, 1917.

The change from prison to the liberty of tongue and mind and pen—by the latter I mean access to news, periodicals, etc.—is too big to be accommodated all at once by semi-dormant organs and senses. Though our bodies are such close prisoners—shut up in these little dark boxes, and closely guarded whenever we leave them to wash, for exercise, etc., it is curious how any realization of bodily restriction is entirely absent. This is because the other liberty, of which I have spoken, is so tremendous in comparison. It brings home to one how, under the present penal system, mind as well as body is straitly confined—(*soul*, of course, never). And perhaps this makes imprisonment to-day less disproportionate in suffering to that of our Quaker forefathers, who, though under so much worse material conditions, had as a rule, a larger mental freedom, I believe. . . . I shall go to the "reading out" with a heart beating considerably with excitement. The officers seemed so sympathetic that if ever there was a chance of getting consideration, it was at this third D.C.M., I think. And the difference it would make in my form of service for the months and years now unfolding is so vast that one cannot reflect upon it with indifference. Yet I never felt such a glorious assurance that, whatever happens, the path of duty opening up will be the right one for me to enter, and that I can and shall enter it with supreme confidence and peace of mind.

EDITOR'S NOTE.—A few days later, when the "reading out" took place, C.C. found that he had been sentenced to a further six months' imprisonment in the third division with "hard labour". Writing of the occasion, he said :

October 23rd, 1917.

I feel it is in the nature of a victory, and the fact that the men came round with congratulations is a sign that they felt so too. One doesn't usually congratulate a man on "six months' hard"—it was relatively to what they had been expecting for our fate. . . . I confess to having had little times of eagerness at the thought of bare possibilities of more active service even this winter. French trenches and *postes de secours* with a *carte blanche* to go just where the need of ambulance help, comforts for wounded, spiritual ministrations were needed. Now it remains but a dream to be dreamed in a little cell, not lived under the clouds or sun, and stars by night, amidst the mud and blood and guns. But my one desire is to serve the cause.

D.C.M. No. 4

EDITOR'S NOTE.—On October 26th, 1917, C.C. was taken from Harwich under military escort to Ipswich Prison. On completion of his six months' sentence he was again released and returned to Harwich on Saturday, March 23rd, 1918. The terrific drama then playing out on the Western Front filled all his thoughts, and made detention a difficult time in many ways. He appeared again before court-martial on the following Thursday, and realizing what the strain upon the military authorities must be at such a crisis he was unwilling to press his own case. He therefore made only a brief statement, explaining his reason for so doing, and expressing his longing to be at the front giving what service he might to the relief of suffering and touch of human sympathy were it possible to do so without compromise with a Military Service Act. The impulse to return to this work of healing, he said, was at times almost irresistible, but " May God steady me and keep me faithful to a call I have heard above the roar of the guns."

When two days later he was " read out " again he was wearing for the first time his " Mons Ribbon ", which had been awarded him by the War Office in recognition of his work with the F.A.U. in 1914. On receiving the ribbon, C.C. had written :

" It is an honour to have been able to succour the wounded and suffering, and in so far as the ribbon symbolizes *that* (which *for me*, to some extent it does) it is precious and I value it. But I hold it a greater honour to have been called to witness for the cause of Peace, and for that I shall receive no ribbon."

IN DETENTION CELLS AT DOVERCOURT

The Hutments,
Dovercourt.
Easter Sunday, 1918.

MY DEAR FRIENDS,

After the silence and gloom of Prison, I was bewildered by the animation of the streets on my discharge a week ago. Little there seemed to indicate the Great War. The scene was so *mouvementé*, the sunshine so brilliant, that to a released prisoner it had almost the appearance of a gala day; but this was probably largely a matter of contrast.

My first step, as usual, was to get shaved. The sergeant was a gentlemanly fellow, and sat reading the paper meanwhile. Invited by the barber to take his turn in the chair vacated by another patient, he explained : " Oh, I'm waiting for my friend." Tommy is always a good sort ; but this was charming, unlooked for delicacy.

It was some time before the haphazard of our causerie threw up the Great Battle that had broken out two days before in France. In the semi-ignorance of Prison, I had been cherishing a fond hope that the great inactivity meant negotiations behind the scenes. It was a cruel shock. Coming out of the gloomy prison precincts, the sunshine had expanded my whole nature with a sense of joy. Now its very light and warmth seemed to turn me faint. Arrived at Barracks towards evening, I was taken to the Q.M.'s store, and told to settle down for the night.

This store is the *locus in quo* of the " legal order " to be fitted with clothing and necessaries ; and I assume one passes the night there so that all may be ready against the morning. Q.M. sergt. was out, but his assistant, an old boy who despite liquor restrictions, had succeeded in getting tolerably drunk, thought it up to him to entertain me. Having no use for tea himself, he first offered me his billy-can filled with a poisonous brew of the same ; then he showed me soiled crumpled photo post cards of his seven sons in khaki, and asked me to pick out each one in an old family group, where the eldest appeared in knickers and the youngest in arms. Fortunately he was not in a state to criticize my discrimination—in fact, he seemed to be out for information, and readily accepted my decisions. Meantime he kept recommending me to " Be a b——y man and put them on "—meaning the uniform, invariably tempered immediately with " Good luck to you—you gor' y'r own convictions ; nothing to do with me." Then we had the " 'Gyptian Campaign of '82 " again, which I had heard in great detail from the same raconteur six months before. At last the Q.M. sergt. came in, bluff and good natured. He took me outside to feel the air-vibrations caused by gunfire in France. (Drunk and I had been locked in, previously.) Then we turned in, and before going to sleep, he called out to me to be sure to wake him at 6.30, as he had important work to do before reveillé. The Q.M. store is not a bad place for the night, as it contains some thousands of mattresses and blankets, which one can use *ad lib*. This advantage was neutralized by a mangy hound, the property of my tipsy friend (who was still exhorting me to be a b——y man, at the top of his voice in his sleep). The hound persisted in coiling himself up on my bed. I remembered vividly the irritating sequel of similar attentions on a previous occasion, and spent most of the night in throwing him off by the scruff of the neck, countered by his marvellous canine patience in returning, more in sorrow than in anger, to the old position.

When cracks in the shutters showed about as much light as greets the 5.30 waking Prison bell, I arose and poked my sergeant. He rolled over with an indignant snort. I suggested it was 6.30. He said it was no such thing. I reminded him (I had heard a casual remark about it the day before) that summer time had begun. He said no, it began to-morrow, and rolled over again.

I begged him to look at his watch. "By gum, it's after" he cried, and sprang out of bed. . . .

I had soon gone through the familiar little ceremony, of which the final scene is a detention cell. The guard-room greeted me with a chorus of "Stick it old boy", "Good luck to you", "Thank God some one has a will of his own", etc. Such remarks used to strike one, but now they appear so natural that one hardly notices them ; takes them for granted, like the sympathy one meets universally nowadays amongst the men. It is good to be back amongst soldiers again. The army is so human after Prison. As Carlyle says, speaking of the Garde Française in the French Revolution, "However much you try to drill a man into an automaton, there's always a proportion of human being left." It is the cold, calculated system of inhumanity that strikes one about Prison. A few weeks after entering prison for the first time, I asked a friend how he was getting on. It's organized hell he replied— and I thought he could not have described it better. Of course, one gets used to things, but that is the first impression. The men in the army are kinder than ever. Old faces meet one everywhere. A broad grin accosts you : you try to recall where you have met it before. You remember a very genial though smelly individual who shared his blankets with you in a guard-room at the other side of England. With others you hit on mutual acquaintances—A lad from Evesham, who has sat under a good friend of ours in Sunday School there; a co-worker with my old school-fellow who is Secretary of the Y.M.C.A. at Bristol ; a Birmingham Adult School man ; a friend of the Quakers in Darlington, and so on.

The old Provost-sergeant, who is in charge of the Cells, was friendly as ever. "I shall want you to go sick in the morning" (i.e. go to see the Doctor). On the way to the doctor, the following dialogue takes place :

Myself : "Joe, I think I shall let him examine me this time ; I hate refusing. I can't really say I have a conscientious objection to being medically examined."

Sergeant : " You'll give your whole case away, if you do."

Myself : " But it isn't like a legal order, Joe."

Sergeant : " It *is* an Army Regulation that you must be examined before court-martial, and that makes it a legal order."

Myself : " Alright, Joe ; I'll stick it out." . . . " I'm beginning to see we've been mugged," he added later.

Arrived at the hospital, the Doctor, who knows me of old, enquires pleasantly : " You all right ? Want to be examined ? " " No thank you, Sir," and the affair is over.

One night Joe finds me writing at 11 p.m. (Bugler has bugled " Lights out " at 10.15 !) " Lights still on ; bed not even down yet," says Joe, in a tone of gentle reproach. Next morning I apologized. " I am afraid you're not getting enough rest," says he—probably knowing that I'd sat up even later on the two previous evenings ! " Why, do I look tired, Joe ? " " No, but I'm afraid your mind's not getting enough rest." (I had been writing pretty continuously.) I explained that for the last five months it had not been getting enough work !

It is Mr. this, Mr. that, amongst the soldiers of the guard, nowadays—" hasn't the gentleman's dinner come yet ? " a knock at the door precedes its arrival, and so forth. I think I must have an unknown friend in the kitchen. The victuals have been distinctly better than before. Someone troubles to put condiments on my plate, little heaps of salt and mustard. And each evening a bon-bouche has come over for me by way of supper. " Are you getting an extra meal now ? " I asked. " N-n-no, but there's often a bit over, in't Cookhouse." The " bit over " is made up into a tasty rissole or fish cake, with a slice of bread. Corporal ———, Joe's assistant, comes to wake me every morning (about half-an-hour after reveillé), draws the anti-aircraft curtain, and hands me a bowl of steaming tea—a proceeding reminiscent of super-luxury on the occasion of visits to the homes of certain well-to-do

Friends ! The sergeant of the guard one day asked me to lend him a book to read. I said I was afraid I'd nothing he'd care for, but I'd look. This was my Detention Cell Library : *Fellowship Hymn Book* and Weymouth ; Rauschenbusch *Christianity and the Social Crisis* ; *The Meaning of Prayer, The Manhood of the Master, and Prayers for Students* (S.C.M.) ; Otto's and Hugo's German grammars ; Luther's Testament, and Goethe's Faust ! Another sergeant had instructions to collect my " valuables " (Army Regulations). He came with tongue in cheek, and said, " You haven't any jewelry, have you ? " and turned away without even troubling to hear that " the answer was in the negative ". I've had good talks with the men. They take one's part so eagerly that I've sometimes found myself apologizing for the Government in its difficulties ! One lad, three times wounded, and on the eve of going out again, received a box of wild violets from his wife in the west country. He took out a few " for a keepsake ", and asked me to give the rest to my Mother and Sister, who are visiting me. Self-inflicted wounds are very common. There were three cases in the guard-room at one time, one man having rendered his left arm useless for life. They are up to all sorts of dodges to baffle the doctors. I knew there was a lot of this in the French Army at the beginning of the war, but thought that it had been stamped out. They tell me, however, that in France it is constantly being detected and the culprits shot. Another significant thing is the reluctance of soldiers to fight. "One man in 1915", they tell you, " was worth three or four to-day." All the betting at the front is, who can first get back to Blighty. " God," says Mr. Bottomley, " what a race of heroes we are." Men going on draft have short leave, and every time the guard-room fills with defaulters who have over-stayed a few days. There were fifty-two on one single occasion ! They used to get detention or C.B. as a rule, and deliberately calculated that it was worth while. Now fines are coming into vogue, including stoppage of wife's allowance. The men don't like that. In a recent draft of 180 men,

not a single one had attained the age of 19.   This, and the
drafting of low category men, is causing great indignation,
in spite of " Civilization being in peril ".

Late one night a visitor came into my cell and began
spluttering, a blunt, red faced country squire sort of man,
who gave one just a shadow of a suspicion of rather too much
champagne.   I did not notice who it was for a moment.
Then I jumped up, saying—" Oh, you're the Chaplain—
the first Army Chaplain who has ever come to see me.
How *very* kind of you."   Poor man, I'd spiked all his
batteries before he could apply his smouldering fuse to the
touchhole.   It's very easy to do this by showing a front
of irrepressible goodwill.

I stuck to my strongest defences—" loyalty to conscience ",
" simply trying to do one's duty, as a soldier does ", and
the like.   It was a most comical interview.   A real hard
struggle to be decent was going on in him.   He kept saying
" I daresay it's harder to stand alone. . . ."   " I
know you believe you're doing right. . . ." but broke
away continually from self-control into unspeakable (*sic*)
invective against the Huns, varied with " Thank God
there aren't many like you ", and " I must say I think
you're insane ".   He said he thought they ought to take
away our votes, and when I reminded him they had
already done so, he retorted, " And quite right too ".

Then he quoted the words of Jesus about a soldier's
duty.   " Well," I said, " that was John the Baptist,
however. . . ."   He apologized immediately.   Finally
he fished out a tract, toyed with it for a while, and then
handed it to me, saying several times, " But it's really
meant for soldiers just going to the Front ".   I assured
him I was, but he didn't twig.   On leaving, he took my
hand with real kind pressure, churning it about the while,
a sort of outward, sub-conscious counterpart of the
churning process evidently still going on inside him.

Mother told me she had sat next him at table d'hôte the
evening before at the " Alexandra ", and had remarked
the unusual virulence of his war sentiments.

The subalterns have been noticeably more decent. " Who's this fellow? " " What's he doing in mufti? " used to be the sort of questions asked by the Orderly Officer on his daily visit of inspection to the cell. Now it is " Grub all right? "; " Rotten little hole, this " ; " Don't trouble to get up ". My old censoring friend of Raglan Barracks has been particularly kind, encouraging a long chat on Peace views. I was astonished to find myself taking quite a different line—with him of all people— from what I usually adopt in the Army, talking about " witness for Peace ", "spiritual influence", and I don't know what other pure Quakerisms. It was just that I felt instinctively there was sympathy, and he could " stand " it.

On the other hand, the higher command has treated me with some severity. The O.C. refused me permission to have my teeth seen to, although there is both a civil and Army Dentist in the town, and he knew that I had been suffering from neuralgia for the last four months in prison. Also I had the bad luck to get a notoriously harsh Major for President of D.C.M. " I'm afraid you're certain to get two years from *him* " whispered the men, on hearing who it was. And I did (six months remitted by the General). I wore my " Mons Ribbon " for the " reading out "— I had not felt free to do so before, or to mention it ; for it would have seemed a sort of negation of principle if I had got a " wash out " (to adopt the current army slang) by reason of my military service. It has raised a good deal of comment—officers coming to Joe on the quiet to enquire about it—and I think the effect will be useful.

Of course the crisis in France has thrown everything into commotion. A lieutenant, a sergeant and I were looking in the morning newspaper, a comradely trio. We stared as if hypnotized at the map with its wavy line showing the extent of the German advance.

The officer swept the shaded area with a finger—" All the ground we gained at such frightful cost," he said, in tones of blank despair.

"Bent Sir, bent; not broken," retorted the sergeant. I thought that sublime.

Huge emergency drafts, amounting to half the battalion, say five or six hundred men, have suddenly left. It was due to shortage of men, by the way, that the C.O. said he could not spare an escort to take me to the Dentist.

I watched the drafts away, music playing, through my little cell window, the old lump in my throat. "They've got the wind up over there," was the laconic, universal comment on the Great Battle. I was astonished how indifferent everyone seemed. They sit round the old stove in the guard-room, puffing their fags and pipes, reading novelettes or playing cards, as though they had never heard of the Somme, or realized that the "fate of the world" were being diced for there. As for me, I was sick at heart, and my thoughts turned and returned to the battlefield, try as I would to concentrate them.

In the midst of all one's love and sympathy for the English and French soldier lads (it is, naturally, the French that are most vividly pictured by my own imagination) in this time of agony, who will not spare a feeling of pity for the Germans? See the photos of the young boy prisoners (I am told that numbers of those taken before Cambrai early this year were 14 and 15 years old !). Think of them being fed by hundreds of thousands into the slaughter machine, think of their blind devotion to the mailed hands that shovel them forward to die. Are they not supremely the victims of militarism? Do they not cry to us, inarticulate, unconsciously, perhaps, to save them from its awful tyranny? And we say we are out to save them. How? "Every German killed is a point in our favour" . . . "We are killing them at a very satisfactory rate" . . . The final issue can never be conclusive if it is compassed solely by brute force. Tommy just wants the end of the war, and is indifferent how it comes. "Fritz" (that is the word now) is spoken of in a perfectly neutral way—he is just a poor conscripted victim like the rest of us, longing for peace as much as we.

And all the while kindly human lives—millions upon millions of them—are being moved as pawns in the game —losses budgeted for by the hundred thousand.

And what is the "Freedom" we are fighting for, anyway? Should we be free if we " knocked out " Germany ? Would she be free ? No ! We should be enslaved by the crushing burden of vast armaments to keep her down. Some of us have felt, in our prison cells, that we alone are free— soul-free amid a world enslaved. I have seen a vision of Englishman and German standing together, shoulder to shoulder in the fight for that Freedom, against all the tryannies that chain the soul—the noblest cause in which a man can enlist.

I often come to a point in discussion when people say : " You want to preach these views to the Germans "—the French tell you the same thing : " Aller en Allemagne comme Apôtre." Precisely (with one's own definition of preaching) : and that's the only way we or any one else can free the Germans from militarism !

.　　　.　　　.　　　.

For several nights I have lain sleepless, my thoughts out there on the Somme . . .

. . . But little by little there has stolen into my heart, bringing a measure of Peace and quiet, the sense that now is the dark hour before Dawn : that Day is at hand.

For is it not the Resurrection morn ?

CONCLUSION

EDITOR'S NOTE.—C.C. was this time sentenced to eighteen months' "hard labour," as we have seen—a term three times as long as any of his previous sentences ; and now is gone again into silence, with what hopes and fears, in what strength and weakness, we may glimpse in the following passage written as he was entering upon this fourth imprisonment :

The battalion is paraded : standing easy, butts grounded. The prisoner is brought out between the soldiers of the guard, with fixed bayonets, for sentence of court-martial as a C.O. " Parade—'tion ! " Smart click of moving heels and rifles. The Adjutant steps from the Colonel's office, papers in hand. " Prisoner, advance ten paces—quick march ! " He stands alone, in mufti, bare-headed, facing the battalion, rank upon rank. " The prisoner is found guilty . . . pause . . . the prisoner is sentenced to eighteen months' imprisonment with hard labour . . . pause . . . Lead the prisoner to cells ! "

Later, he is at the gloomy gaol gate, sergeant is ringing, two soldiers guard the prisoner. He turns to bid a last good-bye to all he is leaving, the world of active fellowship with his kind, which is *life*. The street is full of traffic— a tram stops—men and women get down. Paper boys run by crying, " Great German push ! " He notices a dog, a pretty little black and tan terrier. The gate is opening. He passes from all that men hold dear, into the silence and isolation, the death in life, where the dreary hours will lengthen slowly into days, weeks and months. . . . He is in *Reception*, that part of prison routine where first impressions are stamped so indelibly on the memory. He steps naked from the last vestiges of the old

life—the little pile of his clothing upon the floor ! Then the
bath, and those new garments covered with broad arrows,
which have grown so familiar. He enters the reception
cell, for those long hours of waiting, till the doctor comes
to pass him for hard labour. A tin of porridge and a bit
of bread are thrust into his hands. He hears the key turn
twice. Weary in mind and body, he sinks upon a stool.
.   .   . What was it those boys were shouting ? " Great
German push .   . ." He has seen the poison gas cloud
rolling over the trenches, the bloody work of shells, the
never-ending stream of shattered bodies. Memories stab
into his brain with unsparing strokes. If only .   .   .
oh, to be there ! To give all in helping to save some life
from that awful wreck ! To ease the maddened brain in
activity of heart and fingers ! .   .   . He starts up,
stares at the locked door, at the walls—they seem shrinking
in on him. He drops back helpless and baffled. .   .   .
Nay, has he not just come out from the base with a new
draft ? Shall the soldier choose the front where he will
fight ? Oh, Christ—give patience to this simple private !
.   .   . Little by little, kind nature dulls the pain, blunts
the edge of piercing thoughts, weaves in others, gentler ;
confuses the pattern for him, and at last applies her solace
for tired minds and bodies. .   . The key is grating in
the lock, the hinges creek louder and louder, and a rough
voice is calling, " 'Ere, get up there ! " —and then to
someone behind, " Blest if ' fourteen ' ain't forgotten 'is
supper ! "

PUBLISHER'S NOTE

THE Letters contained in this little book fall into two groups—
those written from the Front in Flanders, and those from Army
Barracks at home in England. The latter describe the writer's
experiences down to Easter 1918, after he had already undergone
sentences aggregating one and a quarter year's hard labour in
various prisons.

Although each release from captivity was accompanied by
re-arrest at the prison door and immediate return to the regiment,
a certain mental relief, and the exhilaration of changed surroundings, are nevertheless reflected in the Barracks Letters. Over the
long intervening periods of imprisonment the present Letters
jump in silence. They end with the clang of prison gates.
Beyond that gloomy portal, closing again behind the prisoner,
we do not penetrate. There seems to come for a moment the
sense of chill, a light shiver of something. . . as he goes
forward to the fresh ordeal. Then the echoing footsteps die
away . . . the silence is complete. Some readers of the
earlier editions have said that the book ends on a pessimistic
note. . . Is it fear at the last ?

A bundle of old papers, stained by age, often mutilated by the
Prisoner Governor's censoring, has been preserved. They form
a third group of these " Letters of a Conscientious Objector "—
and they can give the answer to this question. Each one of them
was written from within the prisoner's cell, now more than twenty
years ago. Old discoloured human documents, they reveal
something of what the writer himself has called " the naked duel
between human weakness and divine strength in a man ".

*　　*　　*　　*

We hope later to publish a little volume of selections from these
letters, which hint at the swaying fortunes of two years' struggle
in that spiritual adventure. " This that lies before me is the
expression of my sympathy with all who suffer and sorrow at
this time. The expression of my love for my dear country. It
seems little to give . . . I have been spared much—I must
give much. My friends at the Front give their lives in one way—
I must give mine in another. I want these experiences to make
me fitter for a life dedicated to the service of God and men."
In this, one of many similar passages from the present volume,
we catch the spirit in which the author of this " modern Pilgrim's
Progress " as it has been called, after many and deep heart-
searchings, set out at last for the other Front. How the struggle
on that hard field helped to equip him for future service to the
cause of international friendship and understanding, the forth-
coming volume of Prison Letters will show.